RIGHTING CANADA'S WRONGS

The Komagata Maru
and Canada's Anti-Indian Immigration Policies in the Twentieth Century

Pamela Hickman

JAMES LORIMER & COMPANY LTD., PUBLISHERS
TORONTO

James Lorimer & Company Ltd., Publishers acknowledges the support of the Ontario Arts Council. We acknowledge the financial support of the Government of Canada through the Canada Book Fund for our publishing activities. We acknowledge the support of the Canada Council for the Arts, which last year invested $24.3 million in writing and publishing throughout Canada. We acknowledge the Government of Ontario through the Ontario Media Development Corporation's Ontario Book Initiative.

Cover design: Tyler Cleroux

Library and Archives Canada Cataloguing in Publication

Hickman, Pamela, author
      The Komagata Maru and Canada's anti-Indian immigration policies in the twentieth century / Pamela Hickman.

(Righting Canada's wrongs)
Includes bibliographical references.
ISBN 978-1-4594-0437-3

      1. Canada--Emigration and immigration--Government policy--History--20th century--Juvenile literature. 2. India--Emigration and immigration--History--20th century--Juvenile literature. 3. East Indians--Canada--History--20th century--Juvenile literature. 4. Komagata Maru (Ship)--Juvenile literature. 5. Canada--Ethnic relations--History--20th century--Juvenile literature. I. Title. II. Series: Righting Canada's wrongs

FC3847.9.E2H53 2014   j325'.2540971
C2013-900529-3

James Lorimer & Company Ltd., Publishers
317 Adelaide Street West, Suite 1002
Toronto, ON, Canada
M5V 1P9
www.lorimer.ca

Printed and bound in Canada.

Manufactured by Friesens Corporation in Altona, Manitoba, Canada in April 2014.
Job #

To the brave immigrants who came before and who continue to come to Canada to seek better lives. They enrich this country with their culture and determination to succeed.

PH

Acknowledgements

I wish to thank the many individuals and archives who have supplied images for this book. It is a huge task to amass a comprehensive visual collection. I am grateful to those who make it their passion or career to ensure that these images are not lost but become available to all of us who believe that these stories must be told. In particular, I wish to thank Brian Owens, Special Collections, Simon Fraser University, for his support of this project. I also wish to thank Satwinder Kaur Bains, Director of the Centre for Indo-Canadian Studies and Instructor at the University of the Fraser Valley, for her expert and insightful review of the manuscript.

PH

Contents

▶ **WATCH THE VIDEO**

Look for this symbol throughout the book for links to video clips available on the website *Komagata Maru: Continuing the journey,* at www.komagatamarujourney.ca

Introduction

"Canada is renowned the world over for its welcoming embrace of immigrants. But like all countries, our record isn't perfect. We haven't always lived up to our own ideals." This excerpt from Prime Minister Stephen Harper's apology speech to Indo-Canadians might be a good way to begin this account of how Canada went from a country that closed its doors to non-white immigrants to the multicultural society we are today.

The first visitors to Canada from India were Sikh soldiers in the British Indian Army in 1897. They travelled through Canada on their way from London, England, to their base in Hong Kong, where they served the British Empire. The soldiers took home stories of a land of opportunity, open to British subjects and full of promise. In the early 1900s, Indian immigrants began arriving in British Columbia, hoping to make a better life for themselves and their families. The first immigrants were mainly young men, who found jobs in agriculture, fishing, and forestry. Many of the arrivals were planning to make money and return to India, but others intended to settle in Canada and bring their families over once they had enough to support them. Canada was not a welcoming place for Asian immigrants in the early twentieth century. Although employers in the resource industries liked having hard-working, cheap labour, the general public and the unions did not want these workers in Canada. Chinese, Japanese, and Indian immigrants were not allowed to vote in BC. Because of this, they could not vote in federal elections or become professionals, such as doctors, lawyers, pharmacists, and engineers. Anti-Asian feelings were stirred up by racist cartoons and commentary in newspapers, the Asiatic

Exclusion League was formed in Vancouver, and, in 1907, an angry mob attacked Asian homes and businesses in the Vancouver Riot.

As members of the British Empire, Indians had the right to travel to and live in any country of the Empire, including Canada. The Canadian government, however, was interested in attracting only white European immigrants. To keep Indians out of Canada, the government passed two orders-in-council in 1908. One of them required that Indian immigrants begin their journey in India and come directly to Canada; however, at the same time, the government discouraged all shipping companies from providing direct passage from India to Canada. The other law required that each immigrant possess $200. This was a huge amount of money and excluded many potential immigrants. These two orders-in-council effectively stopped Indian immigration. They also meant that Indian immigrants who were already in Canada were not able to bring their wives and children to this country. Despite pleas to the government in Ottawa about the great hardship

and suffering caused to these families, the laws were not changed.

Gurdit Singh, an Indian businessman, decided to challenge the Canadian laws. He chartered a ship in 1914 and sailed from Hong Kong to Vancouver with 375 fellow Indians. The *Komagata Maru* arrived in Vancouver on May 23, 1914. Immigration officials refused to let the passengers get off the boat, which was made to anchor offshore. The passengers were kept prisoner on the ship for two months while lawyers, politicians, and immigration officials argued about their case. In the end, the government brought in a navy gunboat to force the *Komagata Maru* to leave Canada. When the passengers arrived back in India, they were met by British police, who tried to send them directly to the Punjab region of India. A riot broke out, and twenty passengers were killed, many were injured, and hundreds were arrested.

Canada's racist immigration policies and discriminatory treatment of Indian immigrants led some immigrants to form groups to fight for their rights. There was a sense that the biggest problem they faced was the British rule in India. The movement for Indian independence became stronger and was taken up by Indians living all over the world. In 1947, India achieved independence from Britain. That same year, Canada granted Indo-Canadians the right to vote. In 1967, Canada made sweeping changes to its immigration policy and a new wave of Indian immigrants came to Canada. Now more than one million people of Indian descent live in Canada, mainly in the Greater Toronto Area and the lower BC mainland.

The Indo-Canadian community has a long history of political activity, including protesting the Komagata Maru and the fight for Indian independence. One of the consequences of independence from Britain was the partition of the Punjab, traditionally the homeland for Sikhs, into parts of two separate countries: India and Pakistan. As a result, many Sikhs around the world began working toward an independent Sikh state called Khalistan. Indo-Canadians are divided on the issue, but the pro-Khalistan movement is alive and well in Canada. Several Indo-Canadians have become successful politicians in municipal, provincial, and federal governments. They have pressed for an apology to the Indo-Canadian community for Canada's racist immigration policies in the past, and for its treatment of the passengers of the *Komagata Maru*. In August 2008, Prime Minister Harper publicly apologized in a speech at a festival in Surrey, BC. Because the apology did not take place in the House of Commons, some people feel that it is not official and are still waiting for the government to apologize in parliament.

CHAPTER 1

LEAVING INDIA

Early India

Prior to the 1800s, India was a vast subcontinent divided into hundreds of independent states ruled by wealthy men. Its early history is a story of invasions and conquests, great wealth and crushing poverty. In 1526, the dynamic leader of the Mughal Empire from Persia (now Iran) invaded India. The Mughal rule lasted until the mid-1800s. Britain played a major role in Indian history through the British East India Company, a powerful trading company established in 1600. The East India Company was granted a monopoly on British trade with India, just as the Hudson's Bay Company, established seventy years later, would have a monopoly on trade in much of Canada. For the almost three centuries of its existence, the East India Company and its army were an important force in Indian life. Britain ruled India, like Canada, as part of the British Empire.

Wealth and Privilege
The Mughal invaders took much of the wealth of the country. Many lived in palaces with hundreds of servants, in great contrast to the poor peasants who worked the land. This painting shows two wealthy women in a garden around 1730.

Granted Rights

The Mughal emperors lived a life of luxury in India, as depicted in this early painting. Emperor Jahangir granted the British trading company the right to set up a base of operation in India in the early 1600s. Before long the British were allowed to buy land, create a currency, establish a military to defend British interests in India, and become the local authority for criminal and civil actions.

Mughal Invasion

India was invaded by the Mughal Empire in 1526. They ruled for more than 300 years. This Mughal painting illustrates a city being conquered in the early part of the invasion.

Punjab Empire

Ranjit Singh, pictured here, was the founder of the Punjab, or Sikh, Empire in the early 1800s. The British East India Company, a major military force as well as a trading company, viewed the Sikh Empire as an obstacle and annexed it after the British victory in the Anglo-Sikh Wars, which were fought from 1839 to 1849.

Early India   9

Early Sikhism

The Sikh religion and culture were first established in the Punjab region of India in the fifteenth century. By the early 1600s, Sikhism had established itself firmly as a spiritual path that was different from both Hinduism and Islam, traditionally the predominant religions of the Punjab. In 1699, the Khalsa, or "order of pure ones," was created. It was envisioned as a military organization, guided by Sikh teachings, to protect those persecuted under Mughal rule. Individuals were baptized as Khalsa warriors. Although at first a religious minority within the Punjab, Sikhs developed a great deal of military power. This painting shows Balwant Singh, an early Sikh, in the 1700s.

Jagannath Temple

This temple in Odisha, India, is an important pilgrimage destination in the Hindu religion. In the foreground is a gathering of the peasant class, some of whom appear to be suffering from poverty and disease. Although there was great wealth leading up to the twentieth century, there was also tremendous suffering and poverty for the majority of people.

Taj Mahal
The Taj Mahal in Agra is a world-famous example of Mughal architecture. It was completed around 1653.

Mughal Builder
Shar Jahan, pictured here, was considered the greatest of the Mughal builders. He built the Taj Mahal in memory of his third wife.

Market Day
While emperors built palaces and fought wars to gain more power and wealth, most of the population lived in rural areas and were very poor. This illustration shows a rural Indian market.

Snake Charmer
Snake charming, during which the charmer pretends to hypnotize a venomous snake, has long been a traditional occupation in India, as well as in other parts of the world. Governments have taken steps to make the occupation illegal, but snake charmers have protested to protect their trade.

Nautch Girl
Nautch is a style of popular Indian dance and its performers were termed *nautch girls*. They entertained the wealthy Mughals and local Indian rulers, as well as the British elite.

Palaces
India was made up of hundreds of separate states that were ruled by wealthy men, known as Raj, Maharaja, or other titles. Their beautiful palaces dotted the landscape across the Indian subcontinent.

Kashmir
This image shows a palace in Kashmir. In the 1820s, the Sikh Empire took over the region of Kashmir and added it to its territory.

Fighting Back
Sikh gunners are seen here standing by their weapons as an army of the British East India Company advances on them at Ferozeshah during the first part of the Anglo-Sikh Wars in 1845. The British won the battle and eventually annexed the Sikh, or Punjab, Empire.

Khalsa Sikh Army
The Khalsa Sikh Army was one of the most modern armies in Asia in the 1800s. Raja Lal Singh, portrayed here on his horse, was the commander of the army.

Khalsa Soldiers
This 1855 picture shows four Sikh soldiers carrying weaponry typical of the time for armies in India.

British India

Britain and the East India Company sought to expand their power and influence across India from the 1600s onward. The East India Company built a private army that was composed mainly of Indian soldiers, called sepoys, serving under British officers. They fought with local rulers to win land or to impose deals on the local authorities. As their control increased, the British, as colonial authorities, effectively set a new agenda for the country. These measures led to increased poverty and, on occasion, to famine and starvation in rural India. Under the British colonial system, Indians also complained of injustice in both criminal and civil proceedings. There was growing resentment and unrest in the country. A mutiny by Indian soldiers in 1857 led to the establishment of full British rule.

British Presence
This British Residency in Hyderabad was a symbol of the Company's growing wealth and power in the late 1700s.

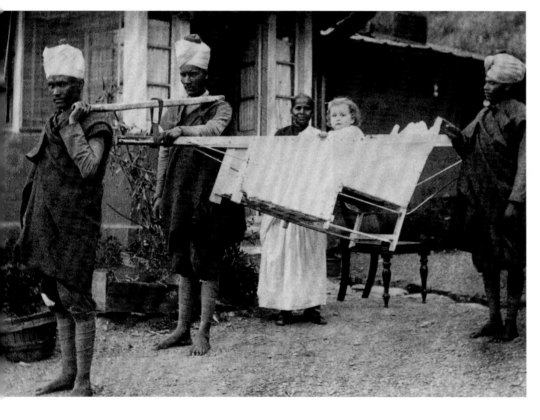

First Class
Many British East India Company officers brought their families with them to live in India. They were able to live very well and enjoyed many luxuries not available to them in Britain. This British child, being carried in a sedan chair or *dandy*, has four servants around her. The creation of a wealthy upper class of privileged British citizens, compared to the poverty suffered by Indians, was one of the motivations for the sepoys' mutiny against the British Company army.

Lord Clive
In the 1700s, the British East India Company was transforming from a mere trading business into a strong military power with a growing stronghold across India. Lord Clive, pictured here, was one of the leaders who headed the transformation and secured Britain's eventual takeover of the country.

The Mutiny

The East India Company army was composed of Indian soldiers, who far outnumbered the British officers who commanded them. In 1857, sepoys at Meerut mutinied. This sparked a host of rebellions, largely in northern and central India. Sikh princes in the Punjab backed the Company in the revolt, as did some other Indian rulers. The revolt was violently and brutally suppressed by British-led forces. The war is usually called India's First War of Independence in India. It led to the British government taking on a direct role in governing India, and establishing the British Raj, or Kingdom, in India.

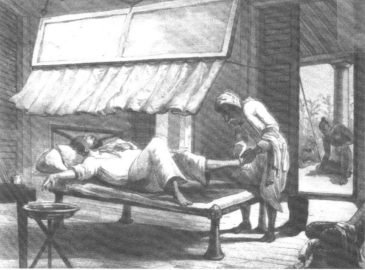

Serving the British

British East India Company officers lived very privileged lives, attended to by many personal servants. In this illustration from the 1840s, an Indian servant sees to the needs of a Company officer.

Early Battles

Prior to the mutiny of 1857, the British Company army fought many battles in its efforts to occupy and control parts of India. Here, a British officer loads a cannon during a battle with Indian forces resisting British colonization at Lucknow in 1845.

British India

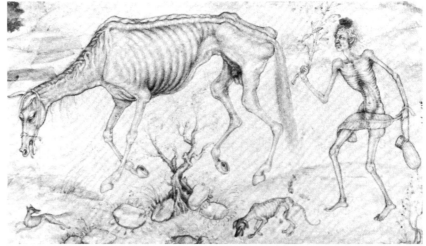

Cash Crops

These young girls are working on a tea plantation in Darjeeling. Under British rule, traditional food agriculture was displaced by the growing of cash crops for export, such as indigo, jute, and tea. This led to widespread famine and starvation in India.

Heavy Taxation

Another consequence of British rule was increased taxation and the increasing power of British-backed Indian landlords over tenant farmers. This worsened rural poverty.

No Help for the Hungry

Despite British investment in infrastructure, such as roads, railways, and canal systems, there was often widespread famine and hardship for rural people. In a famine in 1896–98, an estimated 3.5 million people died of starvation, despite the fact that government inquiries (such as the Indian Famine Commission of 1880) found that there was surplus food grain in every province in India. At the same time, Britain continued to export millions of tons of rice and grain from India every year and refused to lower the price of grain sold inside India.

Famine

Emily Eden, the sister of the British Governor General of India, described a scene she encountered in India in 1838: "You cannot conceive the horrible sights we see, particularly children; perfect skeletons in many cases, their bones through their skin; without a rag of clothing and utterly unlike human creatures . . . The women look as though they had been buried, their skulls look so dreadful."

Child Labour
In order to survive, many children were made to work to help support their families. Here an Indian man and children are weaving carpets in a factory-like setting in the early 1900s.

Living Conditions
A rural resident hauls wood in a basket on his back.

Toward Independence
A poor economy and terrible living conditions led many Indians to leave their country. Others sought to organize a political movement that sought independence from British rule and economic domination. This photo, taken in Bombay in 1885, shows the Indian National Congress holding its first meeting. The Congress became the main political group behind the movement for Indian independence. The British colonial government considered the movement a threat to the country's security, and fought it bitterly.

Leaving Home

When the British imposed direct rule on India, all of its citizens gained the status of British subjects. This status was supposed to entitle them to free passage throughout the British Empire. To escape economic hardship, many Indian citizens chose to leave for other parts of the British Empire. Hopeful emigrants were encouraged by colonial agents and labour brokers who had been contracted to provide labour throughout the world after slavery was abolished. Poor rural people left India to go to southeast Asia, South Africa, and the West Indies. In these places, they found work as plantation labourers and indentured servants. Known as *coolies*, these workers were frequently mistreated through physical and sexual abuse and inhuman living conditions, including forced confinement.

Working in Jamaica
These young Indian girls are preparing rice in Jamaica in the 1890s. After the abolition of slavery in the Caribbean, Indian emigrants were recruited as indentured labourers to replace slave labour.

Coolies

Coolie is a term referring to manual-wage or indentured labour from Asia in the late nineteenth and early twentieth centuries. This photo shows immigrant Indian men and women working in Jamaica preparing rice for export in the 1890s. An indentured labourer is someone who signs a binding contract to work for a specified period of time in a foreign country, often five years or longer, for a specified wage that is often much lower than regular wages in that country. The contract is typically held by a middleman, who sells the contract to the final employer of the labourer. In exchange for signing, the labourer gets the cost of travel to the new workplace — a fee that is usually deducted from wages.

Gurdit Singh

Gurdit Singh left India in the late 1800s to seek his fortune as a contractor. He was disgusted by the treatment of Indian labourers in Malaya and Penang. "I first learnt from a British employer of labour himself that an Indian coolie is not worth even a small fraction of what a horse fetches him." Pictured here is the cover of a book Gurdit Singh wrote about the hardships faced by Indian immigrants around the world.

Mahatma Gandhi

Mahatma Gandhi, 1869–1948, began his political career as a young lawyer in Transvaal, South Africa. He spoke out against the indentured servitude and unequal treatment for Indians in the British Empire.

Coming to Canada

As part of the British Empire, Canada became a destination for Indians looking to emigrate. British army troops, including Sikh soldiers, passed through Canada in 1897 after participating in Queen Victoria's Diamond Jubilee in London. When they arrived back in Singapore and Hong Kong, they told stories to other troops about the new immigrants and many British subjects that were settling in British Columbia. Canada was seen as a good place to start a new life. Labour agents encouraged Indians to go to Canada's west coast as there was a shortage of labourers there. Thousands came from India in the early 1900s. For many it did not turn out as they had hoped.

"All I saw were trees . . . tiny little shacks. Can this be Canada?"

WATCH THE VIDEO

Support for immigrants
This 1908 letter from Teja Singh, Guru Nanak Mining and Trust Company, asks Canadian immigration officials to encourage emigration from India. As a leader in the early Sikh community, he was offering to support the new arrivals. Members of the Sikh community were very active in helping one another succeed in their new country.

Listen to Dr. Brij V. Lal discuss why Indian immigrants came to Canada at tinyurl.com/komagata1

```
C O P Y

                              Sikh Temple,
                                1866, 2nd Ave.,
                                  24th Dec.

Mr. J. H. Hill,
      Immigration Agent,
           Vancouver, B. C.
   Sir:-

        I herewith enclose a copy of the letter published
in the local newspapers, for your kind cooperation and help:-

        "To
              The Emigration Authorities,
        British Columbia & Canada,
           Sirs:

              We will feel obliged if the Immigration officers
of the Dominion Government, send to us every Hindu, Sikh or
Muhamedan (if any) who has not got means enough to tide over
the winter.

              We will give him work or make other arrangements
suited to every individual case."

                          Yours faithfully,
                    (Sgd)      Teja Singh M.H. L.L.B.,
                                Managing Director,
                    Garu Nanak Mining & Trust Co. Limited.
```

Steaming to Victoria
The *Empress of Japan* was one of the ships that brought the first Indian settlers to Canada. An early Indian immigrant describes his first sighting of land as follows, "When our boat was still out in the harbour and we approached the city of Victoria, I thought what kind of a place is this? I didn't see any farms or crops, just forest, like a jungle. Where do they get their food? What am I going to do in such a poor country? All I saw were trees. I couldn't see any big buildings yet, just tiny little shacks. Can this be Canada?"

GERMANS ICELANDERS SCOTCHMEN ENGLISHMEN   AMERICANS   FRENCHMEN   SCANDINA
        BELGIANS   RUSSIANS   AUSTRIANS IRISHMEN

THE MAPLE LEAF | FOR EVER

"NOW THEN, ALL TOGETHER"!

WATCH THE VIDEO

Selective Immigration

The Minister of the Interior for Canada, Clifford Sifton, published this cartoon in 1903 to promote immigration to Canada. A close look at the figures depicted shows that everyone viewed as a desirable immigrant is white and European.

Watch as Ali Kazimi talks about Canada's white only policy at tinyurl.com/komagata14

Everyone viewed as a desirable immigrant was white and European.

TO THE LAND OF GOLD

DON'T FORGET THAT VANCOUVER, B.C. IS THE BASE OF SUPPLIES AND CONTROLS ALL THE ROUTES TO THE KLONDIKE AND BRITISH COLUMBIA GOLD FIELDS.

THE TERMINUS OF THE CANADIAN PACIFIC RAILWAY.

Labourers Wanted

Lumber and railway companies and fruit growers on the west coast needed workers. By the fall of 1906, nearly 2,000 Indian immigrants had arrived, and by December of that year, all but fifty or sixty had found employment.

THE CANADIAN PACIFIC RAILWAY.
TRAVERSING THE GREAT WHEAT REGION OF THE CANADIAN NORTHWEST

A FEW FACTS WORTHY OF CAREFUL READING ABOUT MANITOBA and THE GREAT CANADIAN NORTHWEST.

We Need You

This 1883 Canadian Pacific Railway (CPR) poster is trying to lure immigrants to settle western Canada. In 1904, early Sikh immigration was encouraged by the Hong Kong agents of the CPR. These agents were trying to replace the loss of labour caused after Canadian immigration officials levied the notorious Head Tax to restrict Chinese immigrants.

Coming to Canada   21

"Hindoos"

Karm Singh Manak recounts a story from his father who arrived in Canada in 1906. Many Indians had never seen the ocean or a ship before. When his father and two other men from his village went to Calcutta to board a ship for Canada, Mr. Manak's companions got frightened. They thought the ship might sink. "When they saw the ship moving around a bit in the water with the tide, they said 'we're not going to go on that.' So my dad came to Canada and the other two men went back to the village." By 1908, there were approximately 6,000 Indians in Canada. Although there were Sikhs, Muslims, and Hindus among the new immigrants, they were all generally referred to as "Hindoos."

Newly arrived

Newly arrived Indian immigrants in 1910 at the CPR pier in Vancouver, loading their possessions onto horse-drawn wagons.

Early Sikhs

This image shows some of the first Sikhs, camped in front of Stark's Glasgow House on Hastings Street around 1905. Many were forced to turn to begging for work or money. In 1906, the mayor of Vancouver rounded up Indian immigrants who were living in condemned buildings and relocated them, at their own expense, to an unused canning factory — with no running water — at Eburne, just outside of the city. During an economic slump that began in 1907, many newcomers had trouble finding work. The vast majority were men and they again found shelter in rundown houses and condemned buildings. Many Indian immigrants left Canada and moved down the west coast to the states of Washington, Oregon, and California to find work in agriculture. Like the Chinese and Japanese immigrants before them, Indian immigrants were not welcomed.

Coming to Canada

Queen's Birthday
In the late 1800s, the majority of immigrant Canadians were of British descent. Here, Toronto residents are shown celebrating the Queen's birthday with a large gathering at Government House in Toronto. Note the British Union Jack flag, which was also the Canadian flag at the time.

Loyal to the Empire
Canada's loyalty to the British Empire was reinforced when the Canadian government sent soldiers to fight on Britain's side in the Boer War of 1899–1902. European Boer settlers were seeking independence from Britain in South Africa.

British Style
A Toronto policeman of around 1900, displaying his British Bobby-style uniform.

WATCH THE VIDEO

British Attitudes
Most men in authority in Canada outside Quebec were from Britain or of British descent. Politicians, judges, policemen, and military officers often shared a pro-British attitude. Generally, Asian immigrants were considered lower-class citizens and were not widely welcomed by the resident population in Canada.

▶ Listen to Dr. Peter Ward talk about the general public's attitudes toward Asian immigration at tinyurl.com/komagata3

...Welcome...
IN HONOR OF
Our Soldiers

Vancouver, B. C.

Dec. 31st, 1900.

Homecoming
This homecoming poster was for soldiers returning from the Boer War to Vancouver in 1900. The celebration was likely a very British affair, affirming loyalty to the Empire and Queen Victoria, pictured at the centre of the poster.

Coming to Canada

Working Life

The early Indian immigrant community was comprised mainly of men and teenaged boys. They came to work hard and establish themselves, with hopes of bringing their wives and other children over when they could afford it. Some started out working on the Canadian Pacific Railway and ended up in the sawmills. The forestry and fishing industries were large employers of immigrant Asians. They were housed in crowded, substandard housing and were often paid less than their white co-workers for the same jobs. In the cities, some Indian immigrants ended up working in construction, clearing land for development and agriculture, or as general labourers. As time went on, some were able to start their own businesses and hire others from within their cultural community.

Bunkhouses . . . had thirty, forty, fifty people living in them. That's how they lived then.

A Tough Life
Many Indian immigrants ended up working in the logging or lumber industry. Pictured here is a logging camp outside Vancouver in 1882. Sardara Gill joined his father at Fraser Mills in New Westminster. "There were between 200 and 300 Sikhs. They had four or five cookhouses and different sized bunkhouses; some had thirty, forty, fifty people living in them. That's how they lived then. We had our own temple, a small one built by the mill at their own expense."

Lower Wages

Logging was a difficult way to earn a living. Loggers felled huge trees like the one here, working by hand. Immigrant workers were discriminated against by being paid lower wages than others — a practice that was legal at the time. According to Sardara Gill, "... for wages there was a five-cent difference between us and white people. We got twenty-five cents an hour and the whites got thirty cents for the same job."

Employment Agency

The resource industry in British Columbia actively recruited labour, especially immigrants, whom they could pay less than resident Canadians. This 1911 photo is of an agency hiring loggers in Vancouver.

Building a Business

New immigrants usually started out working for existing companies, but some of them went on to start their own businesses. Brothers Chanan, Bawa, and Nand Singh Johl arrived in Kitsilano, BC, around 1905. Nand's son tells their story. "They got their first contract at Cedar Cove Sawmill. This was for hauling wood. They had their own trucks and their own horses and buggies ... They were the only ones of our people who had a big contract with the sawmills. They used to get the wood from the sawmill and go from house to house to sell it for firewood because everybody used to burn wood. Then lots of our people got into the wood business after us."

Cannery Work
A Sikh man unloading fish at a BC cannery in the early 1900s.

The term "Hindoo" was commonly used to describe any immigrant from India, regardless of religion.

"Hindoo Brand"
The label from this can of Pacific salmon uses the term "Hindoo" as a brand name. The term was commonly used to describe any immigrant from India, regardless of religion.

Worker Housing

The Imperial Cannery in Steveston, BC, provided housing for its immigrant labour. The shacks shown are an example of the poor conditions provided for Indian workers in 1913. Kartar S. Ghag remembers, "When our people first came from India, they used to sleep on pillows filled with sawdust. The one thing our people always brought was their own quilt or blanket from India to keep them warm in winter. They made their beds from rough wooden planks they got from the sawmills, which they covered with hay."

Working in the Fishery

Many Sikhs found work in the fishing industry in early twentieth-century British Columbia.

Clearing Land
In BC in the early 1900s, there was a lot of forest and rough land that needed to be cleared for development or agriculture. Here a group of Sikhs are seen clearing land in Vancouver in 1908.

Ready to Work
A newly arrived Sikh man in Vancouver in the early 1900s.

Working in the City
Although many Sikh immigrants ended up in remote areas, working in the resource industries, others settled in the larger centres. This Sikh labourer is working in a housing development in Vancouver around 1913. Working alongside is little Jack Davidson, who is presumably the homeowner's son.

Clearing the Land
This panoramic shot on the edge of Vancouver, BC, shows a large group of Sikh labourers standing in the foreground. They appear ready to begin the work of preparing the site for development.

Indo-Canadian Life

The majority of early Indian immigrants to Canada were male Sikhs. Only nine Indian women immigrated to Canada between 1904 and 1920. In the cities, the men and teenage boys lived mainly in tightly knit bachelor communities where they could share their language and culture. Those who ended up in logging camps or working for canneries shared bunkhouses or company shacks and kept to themselves, apart from non-Indian workers. The Sikh religion was a very important focus for each community and Sikhs quickly built temples wherever groups settled. It is not surprising that their religious practices, language, and dress were considered strange by Canadians of European background. Different, too, was their cuisine, using many fragrant, unfamiliar spices. There was little mixing between the Indian immigrant communities and their Canadian neighbours.

Father and Sons
Hakim Singh Hundal was a widower and father of four boys, pictured here in 1917. From left to right are Jermeja, Iqbal, Atma, and Teja. The boys joined their father in Canada in 1913.

Starting at the Bottom
When Mayo Singh arrived in Canada in 1906, he began working on farms in Chilliwack. This photo shows the kind of accommodation made available to Sikh farm labourers at the time. Mayo worked hard and saved enough money to get together with other Sikhs to start a business. In 1918 he co-founded the Mayo Lumber Company near Duncan, BC.

Different Dress

Two Sikh men stand out in a crowd of non-Indians, partly because of the traditional turbans they wear. Like many minorities, Sikh immigrants tended to stick together and support one another. "Our people had a very strong social network," says Karm Singh Manak, who was nine years old when he arrived in BC. "The people who were working always made a point of helping those who weren't."

Market Day

Two Sikh men stride across the market square in New Westminster, BC, in 1910. Turbans are traditionally worn by Sikhs to keep their long hair from becoming tangled and to protect it from pollutants. Hair is sacred in the Sikh culture, so men traditionally have beards and mustaches.

Indo-Canadian Life

Religious Procession

These men are involved in a Sikh religious procession in Vancouver in 1905.

Funeral Pyre

A group of mainly Sikh workers in a BC logging camp in 1907 are assembled for a traditional cremation ceremony. Cremating the deceased is part of the Sikh faith and culture.

BC Gurdwara

This photo shows a gathering of Sikhs at a BC gurdwara in the early 1900s. The term *gurdwara* means "Gateway to the Guru" and is the place of worship, or temple, for Sikhs.

Early Sikh temple

The Vancouver Sikh Temple on West 2nd Avenue was built in 1908. Mrs. Dhan Kaur Johal describes the effort involved. "Our elders built this temple by carrying rocks in baskets on their heads to clear the land. They moved huge rocks by hand, going to great pains to level and prepare the land . . . It was a lot of work but they built this temple with pride so that we could have a place of our own here."

First Families
In this 1924 image of Sikhs at a temple in Victoria, BC, a man in the centre of the back row is holding a very small child. They would have been one of the earliest Sikh families in the region.

Male Congregation
A postcard from 1910 Vancouver shows an all-male congregation at the temple. Women were not excluded from the temple, but there were very few Sikh women in Canada at the time. The temple was a gathering place for the community. Historian Hugh Johnston explains, "Constantly in the company of their own countrymen — at work and in their lodging or bunkhouses — Sikhs were isolated by their pattern of life as well as by language, culture, and the attitude of the host population. Family life, with children going to school and contacts with neighbours, would have reduced that isolation, but this was an adult male population . . ."

UNWELCOME IN CANADA

Asian Immigrants Not Wanted

In Canada and the US, especially on the west coast, the influx of immigrants from India, China, and Japan in the early 1900s created panic over an "Asian Invasion." Labour unions were concerned about the high number of new arrivals looking for work and being hired by industries that were already suffering from an economic downturn. Of particular concern was the fact that immigrant workers could be legally discriminated against and paid lower wages than others. These feelings spawned the Asiatic Exclusion League (AEL), founded by sixty-seven trade unions across the US in 1905. Two years later, the AEL opened a sister organization in Vancouver, with a stated goal to "keep Oriental immigrants out of British Columbia." Tension mounted, and within a month came the Vancouver Riot, in which Asian immigrants were viciously attacked in their homes and businesses. Local government appealed to the federal authorities to limit the immigration of Asians and were successful in practically stopping immigration from India. In March 1907, BC took away the vote from all natives of India; they had already done this to Chinese and Japanese immigrants. In 1908, the federal government even launched a plan to relocate Indians to British Honduras, now called Belize. Despite bribes, and then threats, Sikh community leaders refused to leave. The efforts by the Canadian government to get rid of Indians created greater unrest. The Sikh community, many of whom had been soldiers for the British in India, began to push back. Deprivation, discrimination, and ill-treatment in Canada, as well as British actions in India, generated political awareness and activity.

Chinese Head Tax
As part of an effort to slow down or stop immigration from Asia, the Canadian government levied a head tax on Chinese immigrants. All Chinese wishing to come to Canada had to pay a relatively large fee to the Canadian government. This had the desired effect of drastically reducing Chinese immigration.

Asian Neighbourhoods
Chinese vendors on Dupont Street, Vancouver, in 1904. Within the city were concentrations of Asian immigrants, including a Chinatown and a Japantown. Indian immigrants also tended to live close together within the city.

Clifford Sifton
Clifford Sifton was the Canadian Minister of the Interior up to 1905. He was in charge of the immigration policy and was known to prefer "sturdy [European] peasants and not Indians" for immigration to Canada.

Frank Oliver
Frank Oliver, Minister of the Interior from 1905–1911, changed the federal immigration policy to one with a definite ethnic or racial focus. He promoted immigration from Britain in particular, claiming that Canada "had to reinforce its British heritage if it was to become one of the world's great civilizations." At the same time, he levied a tax on Asians coming to Canada, keeping many of them out. Since Indian immigrants had no right to vote in municipal or provincial elections, they were also banned from federal elections.

I thought the word "British" meant Freedom and Liberty!

Bellingham Riot

The strained relationship between Indian labourers, unions, and local residents resulted in a riot in Bellingham, Washington, in September 1907. Indians were driven from the city and many made their way to Canada. The September 11, 1907, issue of the *Bellingham Herald* carries the racist and inflammatory headline, "Horde of Hindus Landing at Vancouver."

Mayor Frederick Buscombe
While labour unions protested the influx of Asian labour, many Canadian industrialists supported it as a source of low-wage workers, putting downward pressure on all wages. In 1906, Vancouver's Mayor Buscombe and the city council passed a motion requesting that the federal government put a stop to the immigration of East Indians into Canada. Without the ability to vote in elections, Asian immigrants had no say and no influence on what the governments did.

Indians Not Wanted

This political cartoon from *The Montreal Daily Star*, March 1908, shows an old Sikh man in BC having rocks thrown at him. The caption reads, "Hindoo British Subject. Alas! I must be mistaken! I thought the word 'British' meant Freedom and Liberty!" Indo-Canadians lost their right to vote in British Columbia in 1907.

Immigration Officials

Malcolm Reid was the immigration agent in Vancouver and H.H. Stevens was the local member of Parliament beginning in 1911. Stevens was an outspoken opponent of Asian immigration. Said Stevens: "We cannot hope to preserve the national type if we allow Asiatics to enter Canada in any numbers." This 1913 letter from Reid to Stevens reports on communication from the Minister of the Interior regarding the immigration of the family of Hakam Singh.

Wilfrid Laurier initially felt that "Canada could not exclude British subjects of any kind or race."

Cry for Help

After the Vancouver Riot of 1907, Alexander Bethune, then mayor of Vancouver, sent a telegram to Prime Minister Wilfrid Laurier, pictured here. "City of Vancouver will not stand for any further dumping of East Indians here. Mass meeting called to consider active preventive measures unless definite authoritative assurances received that government has prohibited importation of these undesirable immigrants." The city council adopted a resolution, stating that continued Indian immigration was "against the best interests of this country." Laurier initially felt that "Canada could not exclude British subjects of any kind or race." He was aware that measures banning Indian immigration would be used by advocates of Indian independence to demonstrate that the British Empire did not treat all British subjects equally. But Laurier ultimately responded to public pressure and enacted two orders-in-council that abruptly ended immigration from India in 1908.

Bachelor Society

The congregation at the Sikh Temple at Hillcrest in 1910, shown here, was all male. The new regulations imposed by the Laurier government meant that the wives of Indian immigrants were no longer permitted to enter Canada. As well as causing distress and hardship for the immigrant men and their families left behind in India, it strengthened support for Indian opposition to British rule in India. The Indian community in North America began to organize support for independence. The temples became a centre for political, as well as, social life.

Considered Dangerous and Unfit

In this 1907 photo, two Sikh men are walking down Granville Street in Vancouver. In January that year, M.A. Beach, representing the Vancouver Trades and Labour Council, told labour activists and leaders, "We in British Columbia have existing conditions which are very dangerous to the welfare of the white wage-earners of this country, namely the Japanese, Chinese, and Hindoo...They are a people totally unfit for the conditions of this country."

Chapter 3: Unwelcome in Canada

Such Is Life

WHITE LABO

ORIENTAL LABOR

Not Welcome

This cartoon from a Vancouver newspaper illustrates the tension between Asian immigrant labourers wanting to come to Canada and white resident labourers who wanted to keep them out. The caption reads, "Oriental labour — If you don't let me ashore, I'll refuse to take anything to eat; White Labour — And if we let you ashore, I won't be able to get anything to eat anyway."

Violence broke out and there was extensive damage to property; many innocent people were injured.

P. D. McTAVISH, LTD.
FINANCIAL BROKERS

822-6 ROGERS BUILDING
VANCOUVER, B.C. Dec. 10th, 1913.

H. H. Stevens, Esq., M. P.
Vancouver,
B. C.

My dear Sir:-

Re the Hindoo Question.

I have for the past year watched with great interest your untiring efforts to effect a proper regulation of the Oriental Immigration to British Columbia.

I have lived for eight years in Southern India and I am one of your strongest backers in the determination that you are displaying to eliminate entirely the immigration of the Hindoo. He is an undesirable and one of the most dangerous weapons to have in our midst in connection with Empire matters and especially to I refer to the Indian Empire.

I sincerely hope you are successful in stopping immigration of the Hindoo into Canada.

Very truly yours,
H. Hen Davies

Vancouver Riot

On September 7, 1907, nearly 9,000 people attended the Asiatic Exclusion League rally at city hall in Vancouver. Following the rally, a mob of thousands marched en masse toward Chinatown and Japantown. Violence broke out and there was extensive damage to property, as pictured here; and many innocent people were injured. These events came to be called the Vancouver Riot.

Support for Discrimination

Local businessman H.H. Davies sent this letter of support to Vancouver MP H.H. Stevens in December 1913. "I have lived for eight years in Southern India and I am one of your strongest backers in the determination that you are displaying to eliminate entirely the immigration of the Hindoo."

Asian Immigrants Not Wanted 41

Roadblocks to Immigration

In 1908, the Liberal government of Wilfrid Laurier passed two regulations, called orders-in-council, that effectively stopped Indian immigration. One required all Asian immigrants entering Canada to have $200 in their possession on arrival — European immigrants needed $25. The average daily wage of an Indian at the time was ten to twenty cents a day, so the sum was overwhelming and eliminated most potential immigrants. The other order-in-council required all immigrants to enter Canada "by way of continuous passage" from their native country on tickets that had to be purchased in that country. That meant that Indians had to buy their tickets in India, leave from an Indian port, and travel directly to Canada. The government successfully pressured steamship companies to not provide direct service between Canada and India or to not sell through-tickets from Indian ports. This made it impossible for Indians to comply with the continuous-passage regulation. Restrictions were also placed on the immigration of wives and children for those men already living in Canada; the families were not permitted to come. The result was an unhappy, frustrated, and increasingly angry Indian community. Their discontent over the discrimination and unfair treatment they received in Canada was largely aimed at the British Empire in general and at British rule in India in particular.

Changes to Immigration Laws

These Canadian immigration officers were responsible for carrying out the new immigration laws of 1908. Although India was not named specifically in the new legislation, the requirement of continuous passage from immigrants' homelands was aimed at Indians. Canadian Pacific ran a profitable shipping line directly between Vancouver and Calcutta, India. When the new regulations were passed, the Canadian government forced CP to discontinue its service to India.

No Objections from the Governor General of India

When Lord Minto, seventeenth Viceroy and Governor General of India, was informed of Laurier's plan to end immigration from India, he wrote, "We hold the view that the continuous passage and the two hundred dollar regulations are likely to prove effective in putting a stop to immigration of Indian labour. We have published the conditions imposed by Canada widely. . . We raise no objections to the methods adopted by Canada, and we have not any intention to raising questions regarding them."

"For hatred does not cease by hatred at any time; hatred ceases by love. This is an old rule." —Dhammapada.

Pleading for Their Wives and Children

REV. L. W. HALL
M. RAJAH SINGH
PROF. TEJA SINGH, LL.D
DR. SUNDER SINGH

Keeping Watch

William Hopkinson was born in Delhi, India, in 1880. Hopkinson was fluent in Hindi but less so in Punjabi. A complex character, he worked as a police inspector in India and came to Canada in 1907. As an intelligence agent for the British authorities, he was paid to spy on local leaders in the Indian independence movement. He was hired by Canadian and American immigration authorities to run a ring of informants to spy on Indian immigrants in both countries. The immigration authorities of both countries wanted to keep tabs on activist movements and individuals they thought might cause trouble in their new home or back in India.

Canada Refuses

In a 1911 newspaper article, Presbyterian missionary Reverend L.W. Hall supports the efforts of these three Sikh immigrants trying to bring their wives and children to Canada. "If they went to Great Britain they could take their families with them. If they went to the United States they could take their wives and children with them. Canada, Christian Canada, refuses to give them this privilege."

Left in Limbo

The Hundal family (grandmother Bishan Kaur at centre and four young grandsons L–R, Atma, Iqbal, Teja, and Jermeja) were stranded in Hong Kong in 1912 and not allowed to come to Canada to join their father, Hakim Singh Hundal. They lived in the Hong Kong Sikh Temple for two years while awaiting permission to immigrate. They were finally allowed to come in 1913.

Waiting in Hong Kong

In this 1915 photo, a large group of young Sikh men are gathered at the Hong Kong Gurdwara, or temple. Seeking entry into Canada, they are being denied the right to immigrate, despite being British subjects (or citizens). When visiting this temple, Gurdit Singh felt compassion for the plight of the many young men. He gave a rousing speech and decided to charter his own ship to Canada to challenge the racist immigration policies.

Roadblocks to Immigration

Activism on the Rise

Limiting immigration to Canada was seen as a good thing by the British government in India. They were worried that a large overseas population of politically "free" Indians might rise up against British rule. While in Canada, William Hopkinson continued to work for the Indian police force by monitoring the activities of Indian immigrants thought to be extremists by the British. Overseas surveillance was considered essential to maintaining British rule in India. The Punjabi community considered limits to their immigration an insult. Sikhs had long been given prestige through separate military regiments in the British military and they had remained loyal to the British regime. The lack of British support was seen as a betrayal. Indian communities in Vancouver began to organize due to fears created by the Asiatic Exclusion League, putting in place protection from harassment from ordinary citizens as well as from police and immigration authorities. In 1906 the Vancouver Khalsa Diwan Society was established to respond to "all the difficulties that confronted the Indians — Sikhs, Hindus and Muslims — relating to political, economic, social and religious problems." News about the struggle for equality of Indians in Canada soon reached other parts of the world where exiled Indian activists were engaged in their own movements against British rule. Nationalist newspapers emerged and activism toward an independent India took flight.

Female Sikh Activist
In the early 1900s, Bhikaiji Cama was an activist working to assist victims of famine and plague in British India. She went on to become a leading figure in the Indian independence movement among Indians living outside of India. She was a writer, publisher, and distributor of revolutionary literature such as the nationalist newspaper *Bande Mataram* ("I bow to thee, Mother"), which was officially banned but widely, and secretly, read by Indians living in Canada and abroad.

Seeking Economic Independence
This is a 1909 share certificate in the "Guru Nanak Mining and Trust Company" in the name of "Soll Singh of Sekha." It is signed by Bhag Singh, executive officer of Vancouver's Khalsa Diwan. Sikhs in Canada were seeking independence in addition to a fair and just immigration policy.

Mobilizing Labourers

William Hopkinson kept an eye on a small group of Sikh men who were working to mobilize Indian labourers along the west coast of Canada and the United States. They encouraged workers, like these men from the North Pacific Lumber Co., to take action against harassment and exclusion by immigration authorities. At the root of their protest was the differential treatment of British subjects throughout the Empire. If Indians were to receive better treatment outside of India, they reasoned, the only way to achieve justice was to work for India's independence from Britain. One activist, Husain Rahim, told Hopkinson, "You drive us Hindus out of Canada and we will drive every white man out of India."

Ottawa Delegation

In response to the Canadian exclusion of immigration from India, a delegation went to Ottawa to meet with officials in 1911. Front row, left to right: Mr. Raja Singh and Dr. Sunder Singh. Back row: Rev. L.W. Hall and Teja Singh.

Leading the Protest

Bhag Singh, a *granthi*, or priest, and president of the Vancouver Khalsa Diwan, joined with fellow granthi, Balwant Singh Atwal, pictured here, to further the rights of the Indian community in Canada. In 1911, the pair went back to India and returned with their families, perhaps to test the limits of immigration exclusions for dependents. As both men were already landed immigrants, they were allowed back in. However, as they couldn't get continuous passage tickets from Calcutta, their wives and children were barred from landing. Both families ended up going to Hong Kong to await permission to land. The issue ignited the entire community in protest. While Hopkinson recommended to immigration authorities that the families be allowed into Canada to avoid radicalizing the community further, their admittance was opposed by both the Women's National Council and the Ministerial Association of Vancouver. These two groups felt that allowing wives to come would help sustain the Indian community in Vancouver and increase their stability and population. In January 1912, special permission was granted and the families were allowed to stay in Canada.

Activism on the Rise

Ghadar Party

In 1913, Har Dayal, a lecturer at Stanford University in California, founded the Ghadar Party (*ghadar* means revolt). Started in Astoria, Oregon, in 1913, the Ghadar Party formed a base in San Francisco and supported activism along the entire west-coast corridor. It was supported by Indian students and donations from local Sikh labourers and farmers. They began publishing an underground newsletter to promote India's independence "because the people can no longer bear the oppression and tyranny practiced under British rule and are ready to fight and die for freedom." They were not adverse to the role that violence might play in gaining India's freedom. This image is from the cover of a 1913 brochure for the Ghadar Party. The party had a large following among Indians outside of India and was particularly active in Vancouver and along the west coast of the United States.

. . . the people can no longer bear the oppression and tyranny practiced under British rule.

Vancouver Priest Hung

Balwant Singh Atwal, on the left, was a priest of the Second Avenue Sikh Temple in Vancouver. In 1912, his son Hardial was the first Candian-born Sikh. Balwant Singh's wife got sick in 1914 and they decided to go back to India with their baby. The British, who were watching all Indian community leaders at the time, detained Atwal when the ship stopped in Singapore and put him in jail. They suspected him of being a revolutionary and sent a letter to the Vancouver Khalsa Diwan Society to find out if he was really a priest. Unfortunately, the letter was mislaid and Atwal was kept in jail, eventually being tried, convicted of sedition, and executed in Lahore in 1917.

Teja Singh

Teja Singh was a Harvard-educated professor who was called in by the Vancouver Sikh community in 1909 to help establish the Guru Nanak Mining and Trust Company. The plan was to create economic prosperity in the future for the Sikh, Hindu, and Muslim community in Vancouver. Teja Singh led several delegations to Ottawa to lobby for the right to bring the wives of settlers to Canada.

The Panama Maru Case

On October 17, 1913, the *Panama Maru* arrived in Victoria, BC, carrying fifty-six Indian immigrants. Seventeen of the passengers were allowed ashore, as they had the required documentation. The remaining thirty-nine were locked in a detention shed to await their trial. In this photo, Husain Rahim, activist within the Vancouver Indian community in the early 1900s, stands fourth from the left in front of Victoria's immigration detention centre, along with some of the thirty-nine passengers of the *Panama Maru*.

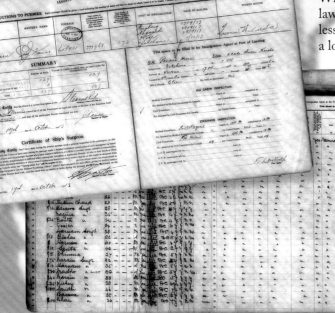
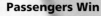

Passengers Win

This document is the manifest, or passenger list, of the *Panama Maru*. When the passengers were denied entry to Canada, they hired local lawyer J. Edward Bird to defend their right to land. The trial took less than a day and the court ruled in the passenger's favour, due to a loophole in the legislation. The passengers were released but their victory was short-lived. By December 8, 1913, the government had put a stop-gap order in place that prohibited the landing of any artisan or labourer at a BC port of entry until March 31, 1914. Before the end of March, two new orders-in-council were drafted to correct the *Immigration Act* and close the loopholes. Nonetheless, the victory of the *Panama Maru* served to encourage the passengers of the *Komagata Maru* to make their journey.

CHAPTER 4
THE *KOMAGATA MARU*

Gurdit Singh Sets Sail

When middle-aged Sikh businessman and advocate of Indian independence Gurdit Singh visited the Hong Kong Gurdwara in December 1913, he met a large group of mostly young, frustrated Indian men who were hoping to immigrate and find work in Canada, despite the rules in place to keep them out. A previous attempt to charter a ship to take them to Canada had fallen apart. Gurdit Singh was asked to help, and he responded. He searched unsuccessfully for a ship they could charter to sail directly from India to Canada. Eventually he found a Japanese-owned vessel, the *Komagata Maru*, in Hong Kong. Gurdit Singh organized a passenger committee that helped prepare the ship for the voyage. Tickets were set at the usual price for the trip. Although he knew the risks, Singh hoped their challenge of Canada's immigration laws would be successful. He brought his seven-year-old son, Balwant, on the journey with him. At three other Asian ports the ship took on more Indian emigrants for a total of 376 passengers.

WATCH THE VIDEO

Hopeful Passengers
Gurdit Singh and his small son, front left, along with other passengers aboard the *Komagata Maru*. "The main purpose of every Sikh is to fight for independence," he had said; chartering the ship to Canada was part of Gurdit Singh's fight. Gurdit Singh acknowledged that the voyage was a test of the British, Canadian, and Indian authorities. He told a newspaper reporter: "If we are admitted, we will know that the Canadian government is just. If we are deported, we will sue the government and if we cannot obtain redress we will go back and take up the matter with the Indian government." The *Komagata Maru* pressed forward, its passengers only mildly aware of the uproar that it was creating.

Watch Professor Hugh Johnston set the scene for the voyage and what happened when the ship arrived in Vancouver at tinyurl.com/komagata4

Gurdit Singh's Ancestral Home
Gurdit Singh was born at Sirhali in the Punjab in 1860. He came from a long line of warriors; his grandfather and father had served in the British Indian Army. Gurdit left home for Malaya in the late 1880s due to the bad economy and famine in India. By 1913 he had become a strong advocate for India's independence.

Setting Sail
After legal challenges and delays by Hong Kong's governor, the *Komagata Maru* was finally allowed to set sail in April 1914 from Hong Kong harbour, pictured here. Officials in Canada had a chance to stop the departure from Hong Kong, but failed to act in time. The ship went first to Shanghai, where seventy-three passengers joined the original 165 on board. In a letter to relatives in India, passenger Nanak Singh said, "I am leaving on the old man's ship." Next the ship picked up more passengers in Moji, Japan and their final stop, Yokohama. The final total of passengers was 376 — twenty-four Muslims, twelve Hindus, and 340 Sikhs.

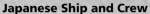

PROTECTING HIS OWN!

IMMIGRATION BARRIER

Capt. Vancouver: "Go Back, my labor market is glutted. Do you expect me to allow you to take the bread from the mouths of my own?"

Japanese Ship and Crew
The *Komagata Maru* was owned by a small Japanese company and had a Japanese captain and crew, some of whom are pictured here with Gurdit Singh. Gurdit also hired a doctor and priest to travel on board.

Captain Vancouver Cartoon
In this cartoon, "Captain Vancouver" is speaking to a group of Asian immigrants: "Go back, my labour market is glutted, do you expect me to allow you to take bread from the mouths of my own?" The cartoon was published in the BC *Saturday Sunset* on May 30, 1914.

If we are admitted, we will know that the Canadian government is just.

Docking in Canada

Along the journey, the ship received a couple of important visitors who gave speeches and inspired the passengers. Balwant Singh Atwal, the priest of the Vancouver Khalsa Diwan Society, was on his way back from India when he met the *Komagata Maru* in April at Moji, Japan. He lectured the passengers on the cause of Indian freedom and the importance of their journey. In Yokohama, Bhag Singh, the former priest of the Hong Kong Gurdwara who had been deported from Canada, boarded the ship and distributed issues of the revolutionary *Ghadar* newspaper. He also gave a fiery speech to the passengers. Upon arrival at Canada's shores, the ship landed at the William's Head quarantine station on Vancouver Island, BC. It passed inspection and was allowed to make its way to Vancouver. It anchored for the night of May 22, 1914, across from Burrard Inlet, and later moved closer to Vancouver, dropping its anchor about a kilometre off shore. Here, the ship was placed under armed guard. Instead of being allowed to land as immigrants or refugees, the passengers found themselves prisoners on the ship. Except for twenty passengers returning to Canada and the ship's doctor and family, no one was allowed to leave. The only visitors allowed were senior Vancouver immigration official Malcolm Reid, and the police intelligence agent William Hopkinson, customs and medical inspectors, and the shipping agent for the owners of the *Komagata Maru*.

Racist Cartoon
The *Komagata Maru* is pictured in this 1914 cartoon in a Vancouver newspaper. The ship is steaming toward Vancouver with a threatening turbaned man, labelled Asiatics, in a cloud of its smoke. The caption refers to Asian immigrants as "all the same" and as "sinister." Negative press like this served to increase hostility toward Asians amongst many BC residents.

Ready to Come Ashore
When the ship landed at the quarantine station at William's Head, it was met by a launch hired by resident Indian immigrants and by Reverend L.W. Hall from the Hindu Friend Society of Victoria. Hall asked on behalf of the group for permission to speak to the passengers, but Reid and Hopkinson refused this request. At dawn on May 23, 1914, the 376 passengers stood on deck with bags and parcels packed. Many of the men were well dressed in British-style suits. One local newspaper story read, "Hindu invaders now in the city harbour on *Komagata Maru*." The general feeling of the public was that these people were not welcome and should be sent back to where they came from.

▶ **WATCH THE VIDEO**

Hunger Strike

The passengers of the *Komagata Maru* went on a hunger strike to protest not being allowed to disembark in Vancouver. The local media were very hostile, and racist in their depictions. This cartoon shows a man with a BC label holding out a tray of food that the turbaned man refuses, flipping the table.

▶ Watch as Doreen Indra talks about racism in the media and how it affected society's perception of the immigrants, as well as the Indian community, at tinyurl.com/komagata5

Making Fun

Published in the Vancouver daily newspaper *The Province* on June 2, 1914, this political cartoon portrays the ship at standstill in the harbour as comedic. The dialogue mocks the immigrants' English-language skills.

Instead of being allowed to land as immigrants or refugees, the passengers found themselves prisoners on the ship.

"We are determined. . ."

When Gurdit Singh told members of the press at William's Head, "We are British citizens and we consider we have a right to visit any part of the Empire. . . We are determined to make this a test case and if we are refused entrance to your country, the matter will not end here. What is done with this shipload of my people will determine whether we shall have peace in all parts of the British Empire." For many Indians, this was a test of the true value of their status as British subjects. Advocates of Indian independence saw it as proof that all British subjects were not equal.

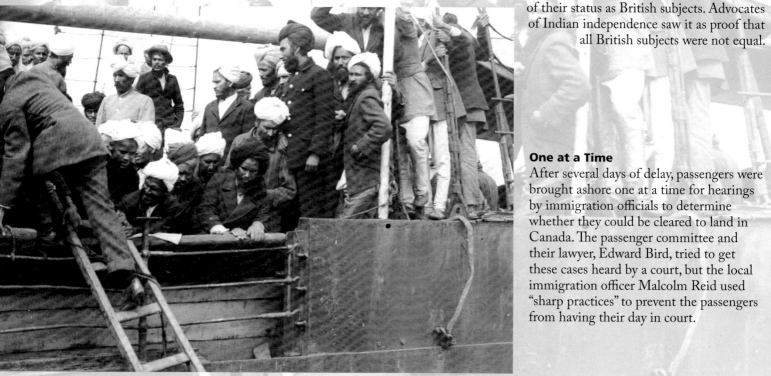

One at a Time

After several days of delay, passengers were brought ashore one at a time for hearings by immigration officials to determine whether they could be cleared to land in Canada. The passenger committee and their lawyer, Edward Bird, tried to get these cases heard by a court, but the local immigration officer Malcolm Reid used "sharp practices" to prevent the passengers from having their day in court.

Will the Dyke Hold?

The dyke in this cartoon represents Canada's immigration laws , portrayed as protecting Canada from the menacing turbaned man in the waves. The cartoon was published in the *Vancouver Sun* on June 26, 1914. Images like this reinforced the hostility and fears of people in BC regarding Asian immigration.

Speaking to the Press

Gurdit Singh was prevented from speaking to the press in Vancouver, but immigration officials did. Here, two reporters (on the left) speak to Vancouver MP H. H. Harry Stevens (wearing white hat) and police agent William Hopkinson (far right), while the federal government's Vancouver immigration officer Malcom Reid (third from left) looks on.

Sightseeing

The *Komagata Maru* can be seen in the background. Small boats full of locals came out to get a closer look at the ship that was attracting so much attention in Burrard Inlet, Vancouver.

Passenger List

Who were the passengers on the *Komagata Maru*? This question has challenged historians for decades because there has never been one definitive list. Instead, what exists are multiple passenger lists, with varying degrees of authenticity, that feature inconsistencies in everything from the spelling of passengers' names to places of origin. Compiling a definitive list is even more difficult because some of the original ship's documents and manifests have been lost. This manifest, created by researchers, attempts to put the pieces together.

Docking in Canada   53

Hungry and Restless

Canadian authorities refused to provide food and water to the *Komagata Maru* passengers for two weeks after the ship's landing. The processing of each passenger was so slow, the passengers grew restless and desperate. Fights over water broke out on board with the Japanese crew, and threats were made on Gurdit Singh's life. Vancouver lawyer Edward Bird was hired by a special "shore committee" that had been organized by the Vancouver Indian community to represent the 376 passengers. He was not allowed on board the ship to speak with the people he was representing. Immigration officials permitted only letters back and forth. Edward Bird reported to his superiors in Ottawa: "Gurdit Singh is even more a prisoner than if he were in a penitentiary."

A Proposal

Through his lawyer Edward Bird, Gurdit Singh, seen here in the background with arms raised, proposed that a detention shed be provided for the *Komagata Maru*'s passengers at his expense, and that the ship be released back to its Hong Kong owners. All passengers could then be detained ashore, subject to their deportation or admittance to Canada. Immigration official Malcolm Reid strongly opposed this idea, claiming to be afraid of white riots should the passengers be allowed on shore.

Big Attraction

A huge crowd of curious local residents and reporters gathered in Vancouver to watch the *Komagata Maru* situation unfold.

Chapter 4: The *Komagata Maru*

ਜਹਾਜ਼ ਦਾ ਸਫ਼ਰ

[ਇਸ ਪੰਨੇ ਉੱਤੇ ਗੁਰਮੁਖੀ ਵਿੱਚ ਹੱਥ-ਲਿਖਤ ਪਾਠ ਹੈ]

"It is not about 376 Hindustanis on the ship but the fate of 330 million Indians..do not send less than 5 dollars please"

Fundraising on Shore

With demands for fees from the shipping agent mounting, leaders of the Vancouver Sikh community, Bhag Singh and Rahim Singh, organized an appeal to collect money from the Indian community. A meeting at the end of May 1914 was attended by more than 500 community members. They called for a return of the spirit of 1857 (the Mutiny), the need for unity against the British, and the inevitability of revolution if India did not gain self-rule within a few years.

Gurdit Singh wrote that William Hopkinson asked for a bribe of 2,000 pounds to solve the issue.

Private Meeting

As they waited in Vancouver, Gurdit Singh related that police agent William Hopkinson, shown in the centre of photo, above ladder, asked to meet privately with him. In his journal, Gurdit Singh wrote that Hopkinson asked for a bribe of 2,000 pounds to solve the issue. "Mr. Hopkinson held out that this was the only way open to us for effecting our landing and I agreed to relieve the sufferings of the passengers. I was to hand over to him an earnest of 1,000 pounds in gold, the remainder to be paid when all my passengers had landed." Hopkinson wanted Singh to swear on the Sikh holy book that he would not mention the deal to anybody. Singh refused since he would have to ask the community for the money. Hopkinson left empty-handed with the threat, "I will see you."

Stand Off

By the end of the first week of June 1914, about two weeks after their arrival, the passengers clearly lacked food and water. Immigration officials, pictured here, sent water but no food. On Friday, June 6, Gurdit Singh sent a telegram to the King of England and the Governor General of Canada via immigration officials. "No provisions since four days. Reid refuses provide. Charterer and passengers starving. Kept prisoners." The doctor on board sent a note ashore, warning that he and his family had nothing to eat and that he was unable to look after the health of passengers aboard. At Gurdit Singh's expense, Hopkinson provided one meal for passengers the following Monday night.

The Court's Verdict

Almost three weeks after the ship landed at Vancouver, only about fourteen of its passengers had been processed. None had been ordered deported. Immigration officials were applying pressure by not providing food or water, claiming that the shipping company and its charterers were responsible for the passenger's provisions. Eventually the shore committee brought food and paid the money owed to the shipping agent, which gave them temporary control of the charter. Despite opposition from Canadian immigration official Malcolm Reid and local MP H.H. Stevens, federal government lawyers eventually ordered Reid to bring two passengers of the *Komagata Maru* forward to be tried as a test case under the *Immigration Act*. The test case ended in failure for the *Komagata Maru* passengers. Canada's right to limit immigration based on race was unanimously upheld by the five judges of BC's Court of Appeal.

Closely Watched
Immigration officials are seen here on board the *Komagata Maru*. While the passengers were slowly processed on shore, an immigration launch with armed guards sailed around the ship at all hours keeping a close eye on passengers in order to prevent possible attempts to come ashore.

The test case ended in failure for the *Komagata Maru* passengers.

Defeated

The decision in the test case was that the passengers could be deported from Canada and denied the rights of other British citizens. The judges accepted the government's argument that it was permissible for the Canadian government to limit the civil rights of citizens, as it had already done so in the case of Aboriginal people, such as those shown here.

Newspaper Coverage

The *Komagata Maru* situation was heavily covered in local press. In these three articles from the end of June 1914, a variety of quotes indicate the drama that was unfolding: "The Sikhs are an obstinate race . . .", "Gurdit Singh's life is in danger from passengers . . ." One article reports on various municipal meetings held in support of the exclusion of Indians. "Send the passengers to Ottawa if they are allowed to disembark . . ."

Shore Committee Provides Support

Members of the Indian shore committee are seen here with an immigration official. The shore committee raised money in the Indian immigrant community to pay for the charter costs, food, and supplies for the passengers. They spent more than $70,000 (in 1914 dollars) to support the potential immigrants during the two months of their forced confinement on the ship.

Forced to Leave

Following the court decision, the *Komagata Maru* was ordered to leave with its passengers on board. Gurdit Singh refused to sail without adequate food and water, the removal of garbage, and proper sanitation onboard. By Friday, July 17, 1914, the *Komagata Maru* was cleared to leave. The ship was supplied with water but no food. The ship's doctor, Raghunath Singh, along with his family and twenty-two other passengers who were former residents of Canada, were allowed to come ashore to stay. That evening, the passengers on board would not let the ship's captain sail until food was provided. The police and the military were called in, and the confrontation escalated into violence. Finally, Prime Minister Borden sent a man to negotiate a settlement. Once food was provided, the passengers agreed to leave. On July 23, 1914, the *Komagata Maru* raised anchor and left Vancouver under an armed escort.

AS IT MIGHT HAVE BEEN
What if a lump of coal had hit our navy!

Fighting Back

Hard-line government officials decided to use force to take control of the ship and require it to depart. The authorities gathered more than 150 police and officials, armed with batons, revolvers, and rifles. They boarded the tugboat *Sea Lion* at one o'clock a.m. The passengers fought back, hurling lumps of coal, bricks, and other debris at the tugboat when it tied up alongside and police attempted to board the ship. Fifteen minutes after tying up to the *Komagata Maru*, the tug retreated. The passengers cheered their victory.

Brick Thrown at *Sea Lion*

This brick was one of the weapons used by passengers of the *Komagata Maru* to repel the *Sea Lion*. Officials were trying to force the ship to leave before it was supplied with food for the voyage.

Going for Guns

During the stalemate between the government and the *Komagata Maru*, several Sikh men were arrested on both sides of the BC–Washington border bringing guns and ammunition into Canada. One man, Mewa Singh, was known to police as an activist promoting Indian independence. This letter from Malcolm Reid warned officials about the arrests of Harnam Singh (activist from Victoria), Balwant Singh (Vancouver priest and activist), and Bhag Singh (former priest of the Hong Kong Gurdwara and now an activist and priest at Vancouver's Khalsa Diwan Society). They had been caught carrying revolvers and ammunition and were jailed in Washington. Officials concluded that the weapons were destined for the passengers of the *Komagata Maru*.

Hard-line government officials decided to use force to take control of the ship and require it to depart.

Under Guard

This panoramic image of Vancouver Harbour shows the *Komagata Maru* completely surrounded by boats. The naval warship HMCS *Rainbow*, anchored a few hundred metres from the *Komagata Maru*, and patrolling immigration launches and the *Sea Lion*, armed with riflemen, surrounded the ship. People in private boats and launches also circled, hoping to catch a glimpse of passengers and get a closer view of the action sure to follow.

Disagreement on Handling the Situation

Malcolm Reid was determined to get rid of the *Komagata Maru*, even if it meant a violent end. Hopkinson, bottom left, disagreed with Reid's intention to send the ship off in the night. When violence broke out between the passengers and immigration officials aboard the *Sea Lion*, Prime Minister Borden became involved. He recognized that the use of violence against the passengers could ignite serious protests against the British colonial government in India.

Armed and Ready

Armed police, military, and immigration officials were all called in by the federal authorities to force the *Komagata Maru* and its passengers to leave Vancouver.

Naval Warship Requested

Following the failure of the authorities to board the ship, local MP H.H. Stevens sent a telegram to Prime Minister Borden: "Hindus on ship apparently desperately revolutionary and determined to defy law. Absolutely necessary that strong stand be taken and would urge that Rainbow or some Naval Department vessel be detailed to take charge of situation." Canada's just-formed navy had HMCS *Rainbow*, shown here, on the west coast. It carried twelve heavy-calibre guns and had fittings for machine guns.

Threats Made

Sailors and armed members of the military, on board HMCS *Rainbow*. In a message to the Indian shore committee, Daljit Singh, head of the passenger's committee, wrote, "We are ready to die and kill." Gurdit Singh described the confrontation in his memoir: "The warships were preparing for action and on the other hand we were preparing for death. On behalf of the government, the commander sent the message 'Leave our shores you uninvited Indians or we fire.' Our reply to this command was that if Canada will allow us to provision the ship we will go, otherwise 'Fire away. We prefer death here than on the high seas.'"

Chapter 4: The *Komagata Maru*

ONE DARK CLOUD REMOVED

VANCOUVER

THE BATTLE OF "CHUCK-A-CHUNK," VANCOUVER'S FIRST NAVAL ENGAGEMENT

Anti-Asian Propaganda

This newspaper cartoon's caption reads, "One Dark Cloud Removed." It shows the head of a sinister-looking Sikh and refers to the success of Vancouver officials in sending the *Komagata Maru* back to India. In 1913, more than 400,000 immigrants arrived in Canada, whose population was eight million at the time. Asians, although a tiny percentage of that number, were the targets of many people's fears of being overrun by "foreigners." The government pursued a policy of restricting immigration to just Europeans.

Violent Encounter

Federal cabinet minister Martin Burrell was sent from his Kelowna home to Vancouver by the prime minister. Burrell was told by Commander Walter Hose that it would probably cost one hundred lives to take control of the *Komagata Maru* by force. Burrell knew that this would be politically disastrous for the Canadian government, for the British authorities, and for the colonial government in India. With the *Rainbow* on hand to intimidate the shore committee and the passengers, Burrell offered small concessions and won agreement that the ship would leave.

Armed Escort

At the height of the confrontation, the British ruler of India — known as the viceroy — had informed the British government that using military force against the passengers would have "a very bad effect in India." When the ship sailed away from Vancouver on July 23, 1914, HMCS *Rainbow* followed it for 200 kilometres to assure the authorities that it had departed.

Forced to Leave

CHAPTER 5

AFTER THE KOMAGATA MARU

A Violent Outcome

After twenty-three days at sea, the *Komagata Maru* arrived in Yokohama, Japan, on its way back to India. While it had been at sea, Britain had gone to war with Germany. Many advocates of Indian independence thought the war provided an opportune moment for revolt against the British in India. Through his informants, intelligence agent William Hopkinson learned of plans for activists to return to India from North America to agitate for Indian independence. In India, the government imposed legislation that allowed the arrest of any citizens returning to their home country considered a threat by the authorities.

While most of the *Komagata Maru* passengers were men looking to emigrate to improve their lives, their experiences taught them much about the politics of the British empire. They had been shown that their British citizenship did not give them the right to immigrate to any country in the empire. They had experienced starvation and military force used against them. Men who knew little or nothing of politics when they left their villages were returning to India having been exposed to powerful arguments advocating India's independence from colonial ties.

The authorities in India would have been even more concerned had they known for certain that a member of the Ghadar Party had purchased 200 automatic pistols and 2,000 rounds of ammunition, and provided

Death in Budge Budge

Amar Singh Nihang, pictured here, was a passenger on the *Komagata Maru* when it anchored at Budge Budge, India, on September 29, 1914. The passengers were told that they were to board a special train to the Punjab. When many refused to come ashore, twenty-seven Sikh police officers, serving under the British government, boarded the ship and brought the passengers to land. Additional armed police officers were brought in to escort the passengers to Budge Budge, where they were to board the train. A disturbance began and shots were fired. Some passengers were killed on the spot, some escaped, and many were arrested. This poster of Amar Singh Nihang says that he was "arrested at the Baj-Baj Ghat (Budge Budge waterfront steps) and beaten to death and martyred in the Mainwali Jail."

Gurdit Singh escaped the violence at Budge Budge, staying in hiding and then living under an assumed name. He eventually ended up in Baroda, India, as a self-taught medical practitioner. During this time, Mahatma Gandhi and Jawaharlal Nehru, president of the Congress Party, became strong voices of an independent India. Gurdit Singh followed their political movement and secretly attended high-level meetings of Indian nationalists and exiles. On November 15, 1921, he surrendered to police as his fourteen-year-old son, Balwant Singh, looked on. "The British government is very unjust to our countrymen and based on that I have made this the principle of my life that I am willing to uproot the government and establish independence for my country and it is for this I have suffered all kinds of hardships." Gurdit Singh was put on trial and convicted of sedition. At the age of sixty-three he began his prison sentence. On his release, he continued political activities and working for legal compensation for the passengers of the *Komagata Maru*.

them to the passengers when the ship stopped on its way back at Yokohama in Japan. The authorities had heard rumours, but a careful search of the ship when it arrived in India failed to find the weapons.

The passengers had expected to land at Calcutta, and to be free to travel in their home country, but were put ashore at Budge Budge, a small industrial town nearby, and were ordered to board a special train to the Punjab. The new regulations for returning citizens were used to justify this order. Police and a force of 150 European soldiers were hurriedly assembled to enforce it. The Indian authorities were using military force, just as the Canadians had. In defiance of the orders to board the train, the passengers set out in an orderly procession to walk to nearby Calcutta. The police and army ordered the men to sit down, and surrounded them to prevent them from escaping.

James Donald, a magistrate and administrator of the district, took the lead in dealing with the matter. He approached the passengers and summoned Gurdit Singh from the crowd. Gurdit refused to go near Donald, saying he would speak to Donald while surrounded by fellow passengers. A police superintendent plunged into the crowd, presumably to arrest Gurdit Singh. The crowd closed in on the policeman and he was knocked to the ground.

At that moment, guns began firing. Four armed police sergeants fired their revolvers. One passenger, Badal Singh, was shot six times. Some passengers used their revolvers, their shots hitting at least four officials.

Troops came running and were given the order to fire on the passengers. The passengers hid in ditches, behind a hut, and in a shop. Darkness came quickly and those who were still alive slipped away.

Eighteen passengers died from gunshots. The authorities organized a roundup of passengers in the surrounding area, and ultimately more than 200 were arrested and jailed. Two officials were killed.

The initial official account called it "a desperate attack on British officers." But even with a censored press, questions were asked about this version of the events, and the British governor of India decided on an official inquiry.

Arrested passengers were jailed in Calcutta while the inquiry took place. The inquiry report, released three months later, backed the actions of officials in Canada and India. There was no credit given to Gurdit Singh and the passengers for their

A Violent Outcome   63

intention to challenge Canada's racist immigration law. Because Gurdit Singh had bought revolvers, he was easily tagged as a revolutionary. There was no acknowledgement that the police and military were armed far beyond the weapons available to the passengers. There was no weight given to a reasonable explanation of the firing by the passengers — that they were acting in self-defence.

Gurdit Singh went into hiding right after the shooting at Budge Budge, and remained a wanted man for several years.

Several thousand Sikhs returned to India from Canada and the United States in 1914–15, many ready for action to support Indian independence. The government investigated them all, jailed a few who were considered leaders, and watched the others.

A plan was hatched for an armed revolt against the government, but government spies and informants were active, and the planned revolt did not occur. Instead, more than 150 men were charged with conspiracy and other offences. Two years later, twenty of the accused had been convicted and hung, seventy-six were exiled to a convict colony for life, and another fifty-eight had been convicted.

Inquiry report
Pages from the report of the Indian government's 1915 inquiry into the Komagata Maru incident and the attack by police and soldiers on the returning passengers.

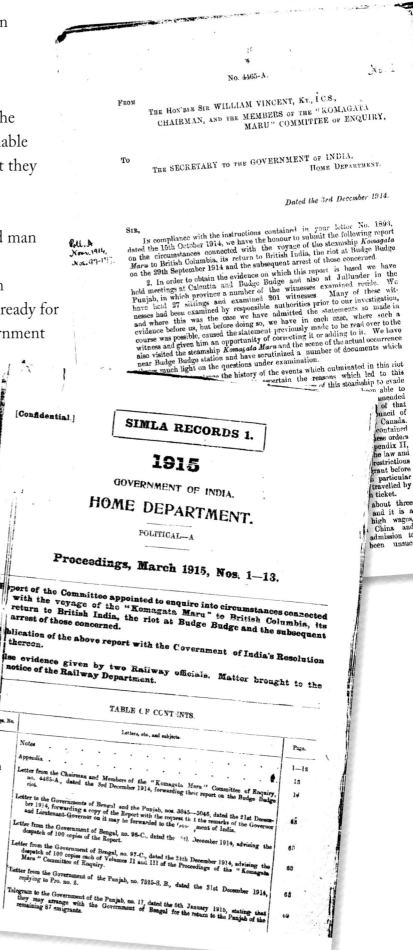

In Canada, a series of murders of informants and activists in the Indian community created great unrest, which ended with the murder of police agent William Hopkinson. Indian police were able to arrest four members of the shore committee that had supported the *Komagata Maru* passengers in Vancouver. One of the four, Balwant Singh, had been very active in Japan and then in Vancouver supporting the cause of Indian independence and equal treatment of Indian immigrants throughout the British Empire. Witnesses said he advocated the murder of Canadian officials and the intelligence agent William Hopkinson. He was convicted and hanged in 1917.

Given the fate of these other leaders, Gurdit Singh had reason to fear the authorities, and to stay in hiding.

Killed in Vancouver Temple

Bhag Singh, pictured here, was a priest who helped establish the Vancouver Gurdwara. He supported the passengers of the *Komagata Maru* by making financial and legal pleas on their behalf. On October 5, 1914, Bhag Singh was shot while at a funeral at the temple. His killer, Bela Singh, an informant for William Hopkinson, was tried twice for the killing. In the first trial, the jury could not agree on a verdict. In the second trial, Bela Singh was acquitted of his crime after his lawyer successfully argued self-defence. An official report by the Canadian government later stated that Bela Singh should have been hanged. Eventually the man was deported to India in 1916 where he continued to work as a police informant until he was murdered by men he had betrayed.

Assassination of a Police Agent

While William Hopkinson was attending the criminal trial of Bhag Singh's murderer in October 1914, he was approached by Mewa Singh, seen here, and shot at point blank range. Mewa Singh had previously been arrested with weapons bound for the *Komagata Maru*. Hopkinson's funeral was attended by more than 2,000 police, militia, firemen, immigration officials, and members of the Orange Lodge. In his trial, Mewa Singh read a statement that said that he believed his actions were justifiable because he felt that Hopkinson was oppressing the Indian community and, as a Sikh, it was his duty to stand up for the oppressed. Singh was found guilty of murder and executed by hanging on January 11, 1915. Ghadar Party literature described him as a martyr. The anniversary of his execution is marked annually in gurdwaras in Canada and the US.

Support for Independence for India

By the 1920s, there was a growing activist movement in the Indian community in BC. They were working to promote an independent India, as well as to gain greater rights for Indian immigrants in Canada. Shown here on the left is K.K. Singh, a prominent representative of the Student Union of Canada. In the middle is Rev. C.F. Andrews, who worked under Gandhi to promote justice for Indians in British India. Andrews visited Canada to express his support for the unjust and racist treatment of Indian immigrants in Canada. On the right is Kartan Singh Hundal.

Families Reunite

In 1918, Canadian Prime Minister Robert Borden was pressured by British officials to halt growing Indian dissent and support for the independence within India it encouraged. The Canadian government changed immigration regulations so that Indian immigrants living in Canada could bring their wives and children to Canada. When the women arrived, their husbands often insisted that they dress in Canadian-style clothes in public. Most young men got their hair cut, abandoned their turbans, and bought new clothes. The Sikh religion considers hair to have high religious significance, and the decision to cut their hair was a troubling one for many Sikhs. Trying to blend in was an attempt to reduce the racism, alienation, and fear that the new immigrants felt from the local population.

Johl Family United
The Johl Family Lumber business is pictured here at Cedar Cove Sawmill on False Creek, Vancouver, in 1924. Brothers Chanan, Bawa, and Nand Singh Johl arrived in Canada in 1905, lived together, and set up their own wood business. They are shown here with their wives and children, who were eventually allowed to join them from India.

Wives and Children Present
In this photo of the congregation of the Khalsa Diwan Society in Vancouver, many wives and children are in attendance. By allowing families to reunite, British authorities in India hoped to undermine the cause of independence for India.

The Social Hub

Jagdish Kaur Singh came to Canada in 1929 to join her husband, the priest of a Vancouver temple. "There were about twenty families in the temple area and the temple was the centre. Evenings and weekends were spent at the temple. We all socialized there, there was nowhere else to go. We rarely mixed with white people, unless they came to the house to buy wood."

Family Time

After the immigration ban was lifted, the wives and children of Mayo Lumber workers were free to enter Canada. Mawa Mangat, who arrived in 1925, remembers, "There were only two families here then, the rest were all single men." He worked at the Fraser Mills in New Westminster, BC. Once families were reunited in the 1920s, the Indian community became permanently established in Canada. Children were born in Canada, expanding the community. A new generation of Indo-Canadians that was firmly rooted in the country chosen by their parents was created.

First Sikh Women Arrive

This official government certificate shows the registration for Mustt Santi, wife of Indar Singh and one of the first Sikh women to come to Canada in 1921 aboard the *Empress of Russia*. The certificate is signed by Malcolm Reid, the immigration agent involved in the Komagata Maru incident. Gurbachan S. Johl arrived in Canada in 1921 at the age of fifteen. He recalls, "Four ladies came on the boat with me so that made a total of eight [in this area] in 1921. Then they came in ones and twos." Mrs. Pritam K. Johl arrived in 1932. "Everybody said that we couldn't land unless we dressed properly. The [Indian] pioneers insisted that we dress like other Canadian people. They would not let anyone dress differently. We had to show that we could fit in and be just like the white people."

Prior to the arrival of children, many people in the general Canadian population believed rumours that Indians had little respect for the family unit and that Indian men were married to multiple wives.

Missing His Mother

Karm Singh Manak was nine when he came to Canada with his father. "When I came in 1921, there were only three (Sikh) women in Vancouver ...There were not even a dozen ladies here in 1923, then they started to come in 1924 when my mother came." He remembers getting his hair cut in Duncan, BC. "Before the war there was a Japanese barber shop here in Duncan. That was the only place that would cut Asiatics' hair as well as the local Indians' [Aboriginal people's] hair. There were only two white barber shops here at that time and they would never cut our hair."

for a
stable
secular
progressive
state

VOTE
CONGRESS

First Elections in India

Once Britain had handed India back to its citizens, elections were held to choose a leader for the newly independent India. This poster was part of the first election campaign for the Indian National Congress Party's candidate, Jawaharlal Nehru. He went on to become India's first prime minister.

Cultural Celebration

These young Sikh boys celebrate their heritage as part of a parade in BC in the 1950s.

Joining In

Three boys of Indian descent sit in the front row of this 1944 Grade One class at Henry Hudson Elementary School, near the Sikh Temple in Vancouver. For many Indian parents, becoming Canadians and fitting in was very important. Mawa Mangat recalls, "My dad made me cut my hair. Right after I got off the ship he took me to the Japanese barber at Fraser Mills. I cried all the way through it. I couldn't sleep for a couple of nights. I'll never forget that."

At Home in Canada

A Sikh family at home in Canada in 1943. Prior to the arrival of Indian women and children, many people in the general Canadian population believed rumours that Indians had little respect for the family unit and that Indian men were married to multiple wives. These untruths were used to justify the prevention of families being united in Canada.

Allowed to Vote

In 1947, British Columbia granted Indian immigrants the right to vote. Up until that time, they had been disenfranchised along with Chinese and Japanese immigrants, and Aboriginals people. The right to vote was required to practice some professions, such as medicine, law, pharmacy, and engineering, so Indo-Canadians and others had been barred from these professions. Above, a Sikh man is seen exercising his right to vote for the first time in 1947.

Families Reunite

Independence for India

By the end of the Second World War in 1945, Britain's empire was shrinking. The United States had fought and won its independence in 1776 and, since that time, colonies with mostly European-origin populations, like Canada, Australia, and New Zealand, had also gained their independence from British colonial rule. In August 1947, after decades of struggle by pro-independence Indians, India gained its independence. The victory came at a price, however. India was partitioned into two countries, India and Pakistan, based on religion. The violence that accompanied the partition left nearly a million dead. The mainly Sikh state of the Punjab was divided up between the two new countries. Independence was followed by elections that made Jawaharlal Nehru India's first prime minister. Gurdit Singh, by then an elderly man, asked the new Indian government to erect a monument to the passengers of the *Komagata Maru*. The government agreed, and Prime Minister Nehru unveiled the monument in January 1952. Gurdit Singh died three years later at the age of 95. Following India's independence, Indian immigration to Canada rose modestly. There was more acceptance of Indians in Canadian society and more integration of the new generations of Indo-Canadians.

Long Time Coming

The long campaign for Indian independence began in the late 1800s. A key organization was the Indian National Congress. Its leaders had travelled throughout the British Commonwealth to speak wherever Indians had settled in large communities. In 1929, the Khalsa Diwan Society in Vancouver welcomed Rev. C. F. Andrews as a guest speaker. He promoted independence and was a friend and colleague of Gandhi.

Two Leaders

Gandhi (right) and Nehru were two leading figures in the Congress Party that fought for India's independence. Gandhi was key in making independence a popular cause for ordinary Indians. He advocated imaginative non-violent resistance tactics to oppose the British colonial government.

LONG LIVE
NEW INDIA
PENDENCE
INDIA
CELEBRATING
FREEDOM
INDIA
WE WISH LUCK
TO ALL
INDIAN
LEADERS
VANC'R.

Celebrating Independence in Canada
Indians in Canada celebrated India's independence from Britain in 1947. A large group is shown here, gathered with flags in front of a Sikh temple in BC.

Celebrating in India
In this photo, Lord and Lady Mountbatten travel in a carriage through a huge crowd of happy citizens in New Delhi. Midnight on August 14, 1947 marked India's independence from British rule and the end of the British Raj. Lord Mountbatten was India's final viceroy.

Partition of India
Part of India's independence involved its division into two separate countries, India and Pakistan. The border of the two new countries ran through the state of Punjab, dividing it in two. Pakistan was predominantly Muslim, while India was mainly Hindu. The Sikh population was split. The partition created a monumental upheaval for many Indians, displacing more than twelve million people. Violent outbreaks, such as the one pictured here in Calcutta, left nearly a million dead.

Welcoming India's New Prime Minister
Huge crowds of Indo-Canadians welcomed Nehru during his visit to Vancouver in 1949.

The *Komagata Maru* Remembered
On January 1, 1952, Prime Minister Nehru unveiled this memorial for the *Komagata Maru* and those passengers who died in the Budge Budge riot. The plaque reads, "To the Memory of the Martyrs of Komagata Maru, September 28, 1914."

A New Immigration Policy

In 1967, Canada made sweeping changes to its immigration policy. The new system was based on points that reflected the personal characteristics of the immigrant, instead of on race and country of origin. The result was a much less racist immigration policy, and considerably more immigrants from Asia. Indo-Canadian communities developed in many major centres in Canada, especially Toronto. In 1985, Canada enacted the *Canadian Multiculturalism Act*. It asserted the rights of all ethnic groups to receive equal treatment under the law. It also declared Canada's policy to "recognize and promote the understanding that multiculturalism reflects the cultural and racial diversity of Canadian society and acknowledges the freedom of all members of Canadian society to preserve, enhance and share their cultural heritage."

New Generations
These Canadian children of Indian descent are gathered on the steps of a temple in Vancouver in 1961. Unlike the children of early immigrants, they would grow up with the same rights as other Canadian citizens.

A New Attitude on Immigration
Raj Paul Gulati immigrated to Canada in 1967. His Canadian immigration document is pictured here. In 1967, immigration quotas for specific ethnic groups were abolished. Because of declining immigration numbers from Europe, caused by the post-war boom in many European countries, Canada turned to other sources for immigrants. A point system was created to assess each potential immigrant, based on their skills and their match to the labour needs of Canada. This allowed a large number of Indians to qualify to come to Canada.

Growing Acceptance
This 1967 photo of downtown Vancouver shows an "India House" sign in the foreground. It reflects the growing acceptance of Chinese, Indian, and Vietnamese communities in Vancouver.

Multiculturalism in Canada
These elderly Sikh farm workers lived to see a big change in society's acceptance of their culture and traditions. Part of Canada's multiculturalism policy states that the Government of Canada recognizes and promotes "the understanding that multiculturalism is a fundamental characteristic of the Canadian heritage and identity and that it provides an invaluable resource in the shaping of Canada's future."

East Indian Immigrants to Canada 1904–1971			
1904	45	1938	14
1905	387	1939	11
1906	2,124	1940	6
1907	2,623	1941	3
1908	6	1942	0
1909	10	1943	0
1910	5	1944	0
1911	3	1945	1
1912	5	1946	7
1913	88	1947	130
1914	0	1948	63
1915	1	1949	52
1916	0	1950	93
1917	0	1951	81
1918	0	1952	173
1919	0	1953	170
1920	10	1954	175
1921	13	1955	245
1922	21	1956	330
1923	40	1957	324
1924	46	1958	451
1925	62	1959	716
1926	62	1960	673
1927	56	1961	744
1928	52	1962	529
1929	58	1963	737
1930	80	1964	1,154
1931	47	1965	2,241
1932	62	1966	2,233
1933	33	1967	3,966
1934	33	1968	3,229
1935	20	1969	5,395
1936	13	1970	5,670
1937	14	1971	5,313

Increased Immigration
This table shows the effect of Canada's changing immigration policies on the numbers of Indian immigrants. Between 1904 and 1907, 5,179 individuals came from India; after the enactment of the Continuous Passage regulations, only 833 arrived between 1908 and 1946. In the first five years after Canada implemented its new immigration policy in 1967, 23,573 immigrants came from India.

Growing Together
Three children, two of whom are Sikh, work together on a class project. The early Indian settlers kept to themselves and had little interaction with the general population. Now, Indo-Canadians are growing up in a more integrated society that respects and values Canada's diverse cultures.

A New Immigration Policy

More Refugees Arrive

Since the *Komagata Maru* arrived in 1914, there have been several other shiploads of refugees who have landed in Canada without permission. Like those before them, modern-day migrants come for a variety of reasons: to make a better life for themselves and their families, to flee persecution, to escape political oppression, and sometimes to avoid imprisonment at home. Immigration laws are different now and refugee passengers cannot be refused entry based on their race or country of birth. Instead, they are detained for varying lengths of time until their claims for refugee status are investigated. Some get to stay and others are sent back to where they came from. In recent years, Canadian public and political reaction to the arrival of a shipload of refugees has been mixed. The Canada Border Services Agency has adopted a more aggressive, stricter approach to these arrivals, trying to deter human smugglers from bringing people to Canada. The Canadian government has also contributed millions of dollars to international policing to stop the ships before they arrive in Canada.

Arrival in Nova Scotia
In the wee hours of the morning on July 12, 1987, 174 Sikh migrants waded ashore in the tiny fishing village of Charlesville, Nova Scotia. They had been dropped off by the *Amelie*, a ship that had smuggled them illegally from Europe to Canada. The 173 men and one woman were fleeing persecution due to the widespread violence against Sikhs that had broken out in India.

They didn't know where they were. They didn't know what to do. They didn't have a clue. They had been 17 days on the ocean.

A Friendly Welcome

When the refugees from the *Amelie* arrived in the night, they were greeted by a local fisherman Vernon Malone, who got out of bed to see if he could help. He brought them to his son's front lawn and waited for the RCMP to arrive. As news spread in the community, volunteers like Rosalie Stoddard went into action. When the RCMP arranged to have everyone brought to the Woods Harbour Fire Hall until plans could be made to bus them to CFB Stadacona in Halifax, Rosalie and others made tea, peanut butter and jam sandwiches, and Kool-Aid to give to the hungry and thirsty arrivals. Rosalie is pictured here being honoured by some of the refugees who now live and work in Toronto. Avtar Sandhu, a Sikh refugee who arrived on the *Amelie*, said later, "I can never forget that night. We were very scared that day. We were scared on the boat. When we got here, people were so kind to us." Mr. Sandhu now lives in Toronto, where he works in construction as a drywaller.

Support and Sponsorship

The refugees were welcomed at the Woods Harbour Fire Hall, shown here, with food and drinks before they were taken into custody. Not everyone was welcoming, though. Although Dartmouth Mayor John Savage supported the refugees, Halifax Mayor Ron Wallis opposed what he called an illegal entry. Some volunteers even received hate mail for their role in helping the migrants. The Sikhs were detained for two weeks or more in Halifax, while the RCMP did a detailed investigation into each person's past. They were detained due to fears that, as one newspaper wrote, Canada was becoming a "haven for Sikh terrorists." Talvinder Singh Parmar, chief of the Babbar Khalsa (a militant Sikh group), brought Mendel Green, an immigration lawyer from Toronto, to represent the refugees and get them released. The local Maritime Sikh Society brought them food and arranged for individuals to be sponsored by Sikhs living across Canada. Once a person had a sponsor, he or she was released into the care of the sponsor until the refugee claim could be processed. Most of the passengers were allowed to stay in Canada. The three men who organized the illegal transport were convicted and jailed.

More Refugees Arrive

Sri Lankans Come in 2010

The *Sun Sea* was the last migrant vessel to arrive in Canada without permission. The Canadian government believes this is due in part to their tougher screening of refugees who arrive illegally. As well, Canadian and foreign authorities have stopped several other illegal attempts to smuggle migrants to Canada.

Refugees Arrive

On August 13, 2010, the MV *Sun Sea*, seen here, arrived off the BC coast with 492 Sri Lankan migrants who claimed to be refugees from Sri Lanka's violent civil war. There were 381 men, sixty-two women, and forty-nine children on board. The passengers were crammed five or more into each small cabin, or were forced to sleep outside on deck. They said they were in fear for their lives if they were sent back to Sri Lanka. The ship had sailed from Thailand and was organized by a smuggling syndicate that charged the migrants between $20,000 and $35,000 each for passage.

A Long Journey Isn't Over for Many

After travelling on the *Sun Sea* for ninety days in cramped conditions with little food and water, migrants were detained at CFB Esquimalt in BC. One man had died during the voyage and several others were hospitalized upon their arrival. According to Canadian Border Security policy, everyone on board was fingerprinted, photographed, and screened for criminality. Although all were released until their immigration hearings, the process was very slow. More than three years after their arrival, only 246 of them had been processed: 105 had been accepted as refugees, 113 had been rejected, and 28 had been ordered deported. The rest were still waiting to hear their fate.

Political Activity in the Indo-Canadian Community

Indo-Canadians have a long history of political involvement, both in Canada and back in India. Many felt that the best way to fight the racism they experienced in Canada was to support the cause of an independent India. Support took many forms, including fundraising, political meetings, and occasional trips back to India to plead their cause or to rally support. Following India's winning independence from Britain in 1947, a new political agenda emerged. The partition of India split the Punjab and left the Sikh majority there without a homeland. Sikhs around the globe began to rally support for an independent Sikh state named Khalistan. Canadian Sikhs were amongst the most vocal proponents, although the community is divided over the issue. Some support a peaceful dialogue about an independent homeland, while others feel the issue is dead and should be forgotten. A small number of pro-Khalistan extremists have engaged in violent terrorist activities that have caused alarm and suspicion in the general public as well as by Canadian and Indian authorities. At the same time, a number of Indo-Canadians have become successful leading politicians in provincial and federal governments across Canada. They serve to make Canada a better place for all its citizens.

Air India Tragedy

In 1985, Air India Flight 182 from Canada, en route to India, was blown up in an act of terrorism. All 329 people on board were killed. The same day, two baggage handlers, loading a different Air India flight in Tokyo, were killed by a bomb exploding in some luggage. Officials believe that Khalistan separatists were responsible for both tragedies. Bomb-maker Inderjit Singh Reyat of Duncan, BC, pictured here, was the only individual convicted in both bombings.

Militant Leader

Talvinder Singh Parmar, seen here, founded Babbar Khalsa International, an armed Sikh militant group, in Vancouver in 1979. The Commission of Inquiry into the Investigation of the Bombing of Air India Flight 182 concluded that Parmar, although never convicted, was the leader of the conspiracy to bomb the Air India flights. He was killed by Punjab police in October 1992.

Local Annual Cultural Celebration

Each year Surrey, BC, holds the Vaisakhi parade and festival. In this photo, participants are seen parading with Canadian as well as Sikh flags. In the past, there has been public criticism that some parade-goers have been allowed to display the logo of the International Sikh Youth Federation, an internationally banned terrorist group. The Canadian Sikh community is divided in their support for Khalistan. Ranjodh Singh, a nineteen-year-old University of Toronto student, was quoted in an interview for the *Toronto Star*, "My parents' generation may have given up on Khalistan but mine hasn't. Sikhs all over the world want it, including those in India. We'll campaign for it always . . . peacefully, of course."

Indo-Canadian Media

The Indo-Canadian media are widespread, especially strong in BC and Ontario. There are a multitude of newspapers, web sites, and TV and radio stations run by Indo-Canadians serving their community. Both the pro-Khalistan and anti-separatists within the community are represented.

Political Activity in the Indo-Canadian Community

First Indo-Canadian Premier

Ujjal Dosanjh, pictured here, was born in the Punjab and came to Canada when he was twenty-one. A Canadian lawyer and politician, Dosanjh was the first Indo-Canadian provincial premier, serving in British Columbia from 2000 to 2001. He was also a Liberal MP from 2004 to 2011. Dosanjh is an outspoken critic of violence and political extremism. In 1985, he was attacked and badly beaten by a suspected member of the International Sikh Youth Federation, a banned terrorist group, for speaking out against Sikh extremism. "[The] young and second generation of my community are being trained in hate and violence. They are fed hate, lies and fanaticism . . . myths of history, not real history, and if you do that 15,000 miles away and you have no contact with reality, you will continue to perpetuate these myths."

Working for Equality

Raj Chouhan has been a BC member of parliament since 2005. He is a founding member of the BC Organization to Fight Racism and has worked hard promoting human rights and racial equality. He has also served as the vice-president of BC Human Rights Defenders since 2003.

First Turbaned Politician in Canada

Gurbax Singh Malhi is an Ontario politician who served as the MP for Bramalea–Gore–Malton from 1993–2011. He was the first turbaned politician to be elected anywhere in the Western world. Before 1993, Canadian law prevented MPs from wearing any headgear in the House of Commons. When Mr. Malhi was elected, he insisted on wearing his turban. Shortly after his election, the law was changed to allow turbans.

First Turbaned Cabinet Minister in Canada

In 2011, Edmonton MP Tim Uppal became the first turbaned Sikh to become a cabinet minister in a country other than India. In 2012 he gave a speech in parliament about the Komagata Maru. "South Asian Canadians have contributed a great deal to our beautiful country. We have worked hard to help build Canada. Things haven't always been fair for us. For decades, South Asian Canadians were discriminated against. At no point was this discrimination more obvious than the disgusting, racist Continuous Journey policies of early 1900s that led to the tragedy of the Komagata Maru."

Political Activity in the Indo-Canadian Community

New Generations of Indo-Canadians

Canada's 2011 census showed 1.1 million people of East Indian descent living in Canada. Nearly half of them live in the Greater Toronto Area and roughly one quarter live in BC. Between 2006 and 2011, roughly 10% of all new immigrants to Canada were of Indian descent. An annual average of 27,000 people of Indian origin received Canadian permanent residency from 2006 to 2012. The Indo-Canadian community across Canada has built temples, special schools, and clubs. Punjabi is the fourth most-spoken language in Canada. Sikh neighbourhoods in Vancouver sport Punjabi street signs and support ethnic newspapers and radio stations. Since 2008, there has been a special Punjabi broadcast of *Hockey Night in Canada*. Many Indo-Canadians have achieved success in politics, athletics and business.

Vancouver Gurdwara
These are the entrance gates to the Akali Singh Sikh Gurdwara in Vancouver.

Vaisakhi Parade
Each year, the Vaisakhi parade in Surrey, BC, celebrates Sikh culture. This float features the private Khalsa school, which offers academic training as well as Sikh religious education.

Success in Business
The Great Punjab Business Centre is in Toronto.

Maintaining Tradition

These two young Sikh boys illustrate two ways of representing their culture. The boy on the right is following the tradition of not cutting his hair, while the one on the left has cut his hair. Both boys are following the tradition of keeping their hair covered. When they get older they will likely wear turbans, a practice that is now commonly seen and accepted in Canada.

First Turbaned RCMP Officer

In 1990, the federal government legislated that RCMP officers would be allowed to wear turbans as part of their official dress. Constable Baltej Singh Dhillon was the first turbaned officer in Canada.

Indo-Canadian Media
This sign reflects some of the newspapers available in Vancouver's Indo-Canadian community.

Vancouver's Sikh Community
This sidewalk sign is for the Punjabi Market district, which is a hub of the Vancouver Sikh community.

Speedy Singhs
In the 2011 comedy *Breakaway*, the Speedy Singhs are a turban-wearing Mississauga, Ontario, hockey team. The movie reflects some of the difficulties that young Sikhs have bridging the gap between their Sikh heritage and their Canadian identity.

Little India, Vancouver

Vancouver's Punjabi Market is also known as Little India. It is located in the south Vancouver Sunset neighbourhood and runs along Main Street from 48th Avenue to 51st Avenue.

Little India, Toronto

Toronto's Little India is in the Gerrard–Coxwell area.

Football Star

Ranjit Mattu, a Sikh Canadian, was an accomplished football and rugby player. He coached the Vancouver Blue Bombers to win the first Dominion Cup in 1947 and later was the first coach of the BC Lions.

New Generations of Indo-Canadians

ACKNOWLEDGING THE PAST

Fighting for Apology and Redress

In 2006, descendents of the passengers of the *Komagata Maru* held their first meeting to organize and obtain an official apology and redress from the Canadian government for the injustice done to their relatives. In 2008, Liberal MP Ruby Dhalla tabled a motion in the House of Commons requesting that the government apologize for the wrongs of the past. The motion passed unanimously and, in August of that year, Prime Minister Stephen Harper apologized to the Indo-Canadian community at a festival in Surrey. However, since the apology did not take place in the House of Commons, many community members do not consider it to be official and remain unsatisfied. In BC, the legislature apologized for their historic treatment of the passengers and other Indian immigrants in the province. In recent years, the Canadian government has funded a number of projects related to educating the public about the Komagata Maru incident and memorializing the event.

Apology

I am a good citizen of this country,
that is what I think, at least.
I drive as little as possible –
our atmosphere you know is already
more smoke than oxygen.
My use of soap is minimal.
We have already flushed enough
poison into our waters
where salmon and
our moral principles float
upside down.

I gave up reading the
evening news.
We cut those
tall and dignified
trees in thousands,
to produce one days' ads,
profits and garbage and some
stories.

I am not the chairman of a
multinational club,
have no interest in starving
all those already starved
children in the third world,
as it is called.
No I don't own a national food chain
either. No healthy competition and
unhealthy foods on my shelves.
Normally I don't even dream of
becoming a premier.

Frankly, I am a simple law abiding,
hard-working man.
And I know what folks think
of me: a boring, straight and
colorless man. Life after all is
ups and downs yeses and nos
soups and spices.

Maybe that is right.
But on one thing you will agree
with me for sure:
I care about my country's future and
repent every thing done wrong
in the past.

That is why
today, on behalf of you and all
other good citizens, I bow my head and
profoundly apologize
for what we did to the Komagata Maru
passengers seventy five years ago.

Ajmer Rode

*Dedicated to the seventy-fifth anniversary
of Komagata Maru incident celebrated in 1989*

From "Poems At My Doorstep"
by Caitlin Press, Vancouver,
1990

40

41

▶ WATCH THE VIDEO

"I bow my head . . ."
Poet Ajmer Rode is the author of "Apology," a poem he wrote for the seventy-fifth anniversary of the Komagata Maru incident. "I care about my country's future and repent every thing done wrong in the past. That is why today, on behalf of you and all other good citizens, I bow my head and profoundly apologize for what we did to the Komagata Maru passengers seventy five years ago."

▶ Watch Ajmer Rode talk about his many forms of writing about the Komagata Maru story at tinyurl.com/komagata8

WATCH THE VIDEO

Looking for an Apology

These descendants of *Komagata Maru* passengers are holding an iconic image of Gurdit Singh and his young son standing with many of the other passengers aboard the fated ship. Jaswinder Singh Toor (Jas Toor), left, whose grandfather was a passenger on the ship, said, "My grandfather and other passengers on that ship were jailed for at least two years . . . We are looking for the help of all our politicians . . . An official apology we expect from the government."

Watch Jas Toor and Rajwant Singh Toor, pictured here, as they talk about their grandfather's experience as a passenger aboard the *Komagata Maru* at tinyurl.com/komagata18

We are looking for the help of all our politicians . . . An official apology we expect from the government.

WATCH THE VIDEO

Descendants of the Passengers Form a Committee

In May 2006, descendants of the *Komagata Maru* passengers met in Richmond, BC, with community leaders to talk about organizing themselves and seeking an official apology from the Canadian government. Tejpal Singh Sandhu, right, the great-grandson of Gurdit Singh, had recently immigrated to Canada from India. He said, "This meeting is the first initiative taken by us. . . We will try to find more and more families and we will form a committee." Sandhu wanted the South Asian community in Canada to unite and come up with a common plan before entering into formal discussions with the government. Jas Toor is on the left.

Watch Tejpal Singh Sandhu talk about his great-grandfather Gurdit Singh at tinyurl.com/komagata19

Official Apology from British Columbia

On May 23, 2008, the BC legislature unanimously approved a motion to issue an apology for the Komagata Maru. "The House deeply regrets that the passengers, who sought refuge in our country and our province, were turned away without benefit of the fair and impartial treatment befitting a society where people of all cultures are welcomed and accepted."

The BC legislature

"Be it resolved that the legislature apologizes for the events of May 23 1914 when 376 passengers of the Komagata Maru, stationed off Vancouver Harbour, were denied entry by Canada"

Fought for an Apology

On April 3, 2008, Liberal MP Ruby Dhalla spoke in the House of Commons. "The Komagata Maru tragedy occurred at a time when our nation had immigration policies that were exclusionary, discriminatory and racist, policies that served to divide our nation and played on our nation's fears . . . It is time to put closure for this dark chapter. It is time to begin the process of healing with three simple words: We are sorry."

Apology Transcript

Pages one and two of the transcript of Prime Minister Stephen Harper's apology speech made at the thirteenth annual Ghadri Babiyan Da Mela festival in Surrey, BC, on August 3, 2008.

Apology in Surrey

Prime Minister Harper is shown giving his apology speech in Surrey, BC. "Canada is renowned the world over for its welcoming embrace of immigrants. But like all countries, our record isn't perfect. We haven't always lived up to our own ideals. One such failure . . . was the detention and turning away of the *Komagata Maru* in 1914, an event that caused much hardship for its passengers, 376 subjects of the British crown from Punjab, and which for many of them ended in terrible tragedy . . . This May the Government of Canada secured passage of the unanimous motion in the House of Commons recognizing the Komagata Maru tragedy and apologizing to those who were directly affected. Today, on behalf of the Government of Canada, I am officially conveying as Prime Minister that apology."

Chapter 6: Acknowledging the Past

Minister Behind the Apology

Jason Kenney, Conservative MP for Calgary Southeast, was Minister of Citizenship, Immigration and Multiculturalism, 2008–2013. He set up Stephen Harper's apology speech in Surrey. Following criticism of the apology being given outside of the House of Commons, Kenny said, "The apology has been given and it won't be repeated."

Presented a Petition

In 2010, Jack Layton, leader of the NDP in parliament, called upon the Canadian government to officially apologize in the House of Commons to passengers of the *Komagata Maru* and the Indo-Canadian community. He submitted a petition carrying 4,600 signatures to parliament on April 13, 2010. "The Conservatives have proven that they have a heart when it comes to saying sorry to communities such as the First Nations and Aboriginals over residential school abuse and the Chinese head tax — now it's time to apologize to the Sikh, Hindu and Muslim communities who suffered from the Komagata Maru."

Funding for Projects

In 2010, Minister Jason Kenney announced funding to Vancouver's Khalsa Diwan Society for projects to commemorate the Komagata Maru incident. Pictured here are Minster Kenney, fourth from left in the front, and a number of members of the society.

Fighting for Apology and Redress

Permanent Acknowledgements

The tragedy of the Komagata Maru and the anti-Indian immigration policies of Canada's past have been commemorated in a number of ways. Memorials, museum exhibits, plays, movies, art, and murals, as well as educational projects for the classroom, are all aimed at creating better understanding of what happened and why. The hope is that systemic racism — that is, racism built into government and institutional practices, policies, and actions — is a thing of the past.

Federal Funding for a Memorial
BC MP Nina Grewal, second from left, and members of the Vancouver Khalsa Diwan Society pose in front of a new memorial dedicated to the Komagata Maru incident. The memorial was unveiled July 23, 2012, and was paid for by a grant from the federal government's Community Historical Recognition Program (CHRP). A total of $2.5 million was earmarked for projects that commemorate the Komagata Maru tragedy.

Remembering Gurdit Singh

The Baba Ram Singh Sikh Temple in Sirhali, India, where Gurdit Singh was cremated after his death in 1954. A memorial stands in his honour there. A memorial to the fatal encounter between passengers and police and troops at Budge Budge had been erected very soon after Indian independence by the new Indian government in 1952.

KOMAGATA MARU

A full length play

by

Ajmer Rode

Translated from Punjabi by

Ajmer Rode
Surjeet Kalsey

1985

Komagata Maru Play

Ajmer Rode was born in the Punjab and immigrated to Canada in 1966. He is an accomplished poet and playwright working in both English and Punjabi languages. In 1985 he wrote this play, *Komagata Maru,* about the incident.

Sikh Canadian Stamp

The Canadian government issued a stamp on April 19, 1999, to recognize the contribution of Sikhs to Canadian society and culture. The stamp was designed by Stacey Zabolotney.

ਕਾਮਾਗਾਟਾ ਮਾਰੂ (ਗੁਰੂ ਨਾਨਕ ਜਹਾਜ਼) ਦੇ 376 ਮੁਸਾਫ਼ਿਰਾਂ (340 ਸਿੱਖ, 24 ਮੁਸਲਮਾਨ ਤੇ 12 ਹਿੰਦੂ) ਦੀ ਦਰਦਨਾਕ ਘਟਨਾ ਦੀ 75ਵੀਂ ਵਰ੍ਹੇਗੰਢ ਦੀ ਯਾਦ ਨੂੰ ਸਮਰਪਤ। ਇਹ ਸਮੁੰਦਰੀ ਜਹਾਜ਼ ਮਈ 23, 1914 ਨੂੰ ਵੈਨਕੂਵਰ ਦੀ ਬੰਦਰਗਾਹ 'ਤੇ ਪੁੱਜਿਆ; ਪਰ ਕੈਨੇਡਾ ਦੇ ਨਸਲੀ ਵਿਤਕਰੇ ਦੀ ਨੀਤੀ ਕਾਰਨ ਜੁਲਾਈ 23, 1914 ਨੂੰ ਮਜਬੂਰਨ ਵਾਪਸ ਪਰਤਣਾ ਪਿਆ।
ਜੁਲਾਈ 23, 1989   ਖ਼ਾਲਸਾ ਦੀਵਾਨ ਸੁਸਾਇਟੀ ਵੈਨਕੂਵਰ

KOMAGATA MARU INCIDENT
75TH ANNIVERSARY

DEDICATED TO THE MEMORY OF THE 376 PASSENGERS (340 SIKHS, 24 MUSLIMS, 12 HINDUS) WHO ARRIVED AT BURRARD INLET, VANCOUVER, ON MAY 23, 1914, FROM THE INDIAN SUB-CONTINENT ON THE SHIP KOMAGATA MARU (GURU NANAK JAHAZ). DUE TO THE RACIST IMMIGRATION POLICY OF THE DOMINION OF CANADA, THEY WERE FORCED TO LEAVE ON JULY 23, 1914. KHALSA DIWAN SOCIETY, VANCOUVER, PAYS RESPECT TO THOSE PASSENGERS BY COMMEMORATING THE REPREHENSIBLE INCIDENT.

JULY 23, 1989

Vancouver Memorial
In recognition of the seventy-fifth anniversary of the Komagata Maru incident, this memorial plaque was unveiled in Vancouver by the Khalsa Diwan Society on July 23, 1989. It is at the Ross Street Gurdwara at the corner of Ross Street and S.E. Marine Drive. Part of the inscription reads, "Khalsa Diwan Society, Vancouver, pays respect to those passengers by commemorating the reprehensible incident."

Memorial Wall in Toronto
This memorial wall in Toronto is at The Great Punjab Business Centre on Drew Road.

The Komagata Maru, at berth two in Vancouver harbour.

The Komagata Maru steamed back to India, where Calcutta authorities stopped the ship and forced it to dock at Budge-Budge, a nearby port. There, the authorities tried to ship every person to the Punjab region. Many were unwilling to go, and in an attempt to force the men onto trains for the journey a riot ensued during which 20 people were killed.

In Vancouver, the atmosphere between the Sikh community and government officials was poisoned. During proceedings at the courthouse on October 21, 1914, Mewa Singh assassinated William Hopkinson, an immigration officer and North West Mounted Police Informer who handled a string of operatives inside the Sikh Community. Mewa Singh is venerated as a hero and martyr in Vancouver's Sikh community. On October 31, 1914, he was sentenced to hang for Hopkinson's murder.

In Calcutta, there is a memorial for the men of the Komagata Maru honouring their voyage and the deaths of the men at Budge-Budge. A plaque in Portal Park, at Thurlow and Hastings, recognizes the ship and its passengers here in Vancouver.

Community Art Project
One of the memorial plaques on a walking tour of the Downtown Eastside in Vancouver is dedicated to the Komagata Maru story. "In Vancouver, the atmosphere between the Sikh community and government officials was poisoned."

Mosaic Memorial
This memorial is found in Crab Park, at the north foot of Main Street in Vancouver. Another plaque can be found in Portal Park on West Hastings Street.

Khalsa Diwan Society, Vancouver, pays respect to those passengers by commemorating the reprehensible incident.

Commemorative Button
The seventy-fifth anniversary of the Komagata Maru tragedy was marked by different events, memorials, and items like this commemorative button.

Timeline

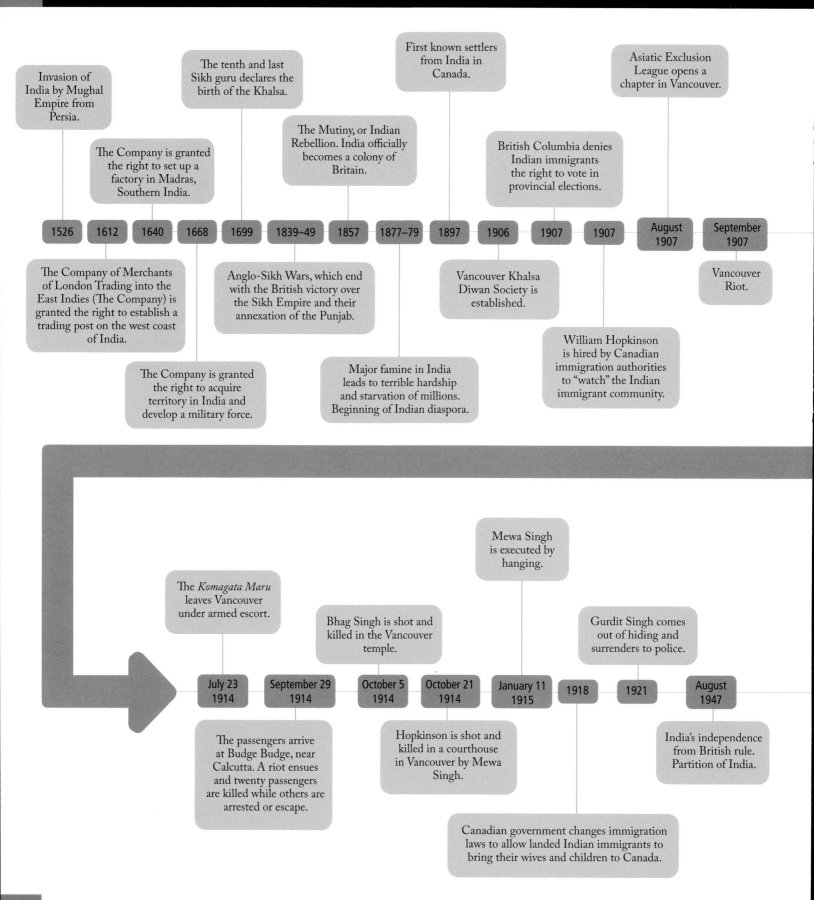

1526 — Invasion of India by Mughal Empire from Persia.

1612 — The Company is granted the right to set up a factory in Madras, Southern India.

1640 — The Company of Merchants of London Trading into the East Indies (The Company) is granted the right to establish a trading post on the west coast of India.

1668 — The Company is granted the right to acquire territory in India and develop a military force.

1699 — The tenth and last Sikh guru declares the birth of the Khalsa.

1839–49 — Anglo-Sikh Wars, which end with the British victory over the Sikh Empire and their annexation of the Punjab.

1857 — The Mutiny, or Indian Rebellion. India officially becomes a colony of Britain.

1877–79 — Major famine in India leads to terrible hardship and starvation of millions. Beginning of Indian diaspora.

1897 — First known settlers from India in Canada.

1906 — Vancouver Khalsa Diwan Society is established.

1907 — British Columbia denies Indian immigrants the right to vote in provincial elections.

1907 — William Hopkinson is hired by Canadian immigration authorities to "watch" the Indian immigrant community.

August 1907 — Asiatic Exclusion League opens a chapter in Vancouver.

September 1907 — Vancouver Riot.

July 23 1914 — The *Komagata Maru* leaves Vancouver under armed escort.

September 29 1914 — The passengers arrive at Budge Budge, near Calcutta. A riot ensues and twenty passengers are killed while others are arrested or escape.

October 5 1914 — Bhag Singh is shot and killed in the Vancouver temple.

October 21 1914 — Hopkinson is shot and killed in a courthouse in Vancouver by Mewa Singh.

January 11 1915 — Mewa Singh is executed by hanging.

1918 — Canadian government changes immigration laws to allow landed Indian immigrants to bring their wives and children to Canada.

1921 — Gurdit Singh comes out of hiding and surrenders to police.

August 1947 — India's independence from British rule. Partition of India.

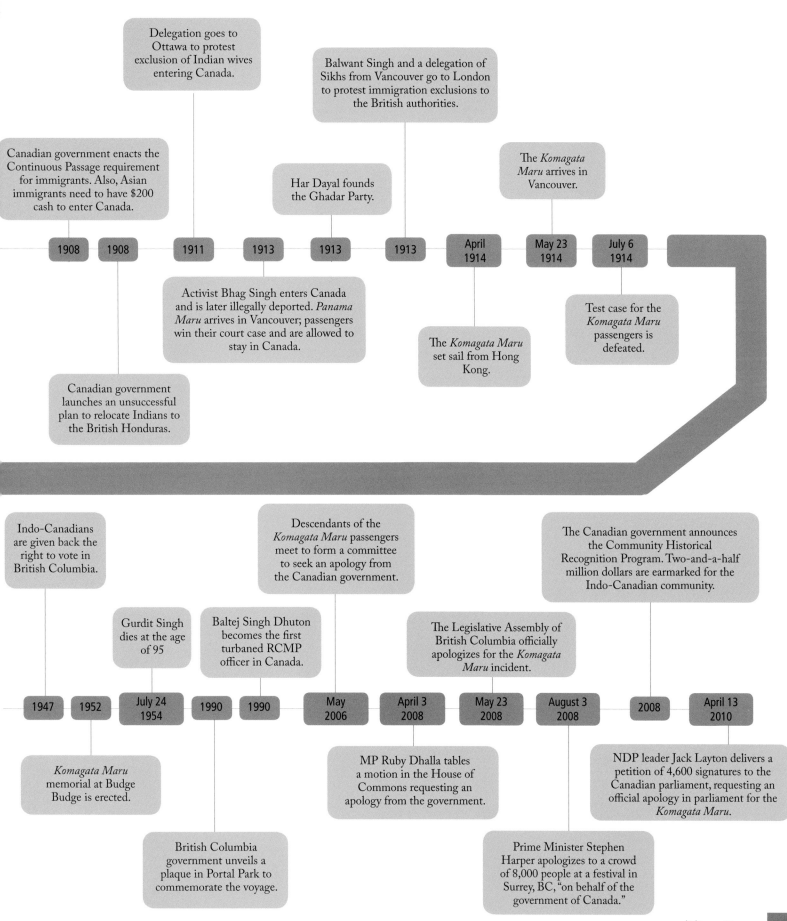

Delegation goes to Ottawa to protest exclusion of Indian wives entering Canada.

Balwant Singh and a delegation of Sikhs from Vancouver go to London to protest immigration exclusions to the British authorities.

The *Komagata Maru* arrives in Vancouver.

Canadian government enacts the Continuous Passage requirement for immigrants. Also, Asian immigrants need to have $200 cash to enter Canada.

Har Dayal founds the Ghadar Party.

| 1908 | 1908 | 1911 | 1913 | 1913 | 1913 | April 1914 | May 23 1914 | July 6 1914 |

Activist Bhag Singh enters Canada and is later illegally deported. *Panama Maru* arrives in Vancouver; passengers win their court case and are allowed to stay in Canada.

The *Komagata Maru* set sail from Hong Kong.

Test case for the *Komagata Maru* passengers is defeated.

Canadian government launches an unsuccessful plan to relocate Indians to the British Honduras.

Indo-Canadians are given back the right to vote in British Columbia.

Descendants of the *Komagata Maru* passengers meet to form a committee to seek an apology from the Canadian government.

The Canadian government announces the Community Historical Recognition Program. Two-and-a-half million dollars are earmarked for the Indo-Canadian community.

Gurdit Singh dies at the age of 95

Baltej Singh Dhuton becomes the first turbaned RCMP officer in Canada.

The Legislative Assembly of British Columbia officially apologizes for the *Komagata Maru* incident.

| 1947 | 1952 | July 24 1954 | 1990 | 1990 | May 2006 | April 3 2008 | May 23 2008 | August 3 2008 | 2008 | April 13 2010 |

Komagata Maru memorial at Budge Budge is erected.

MP Ruby Dhalla tables a motion in the House of Commons requesting an apology from the government.

NDP leader Jack Layton delivers a petition of 4,600 signatures to the Canadian parliament, requesting an official apology in parliament for the *Komagata Maru*.

British Columbia government unveils a plaque in Portal Park to commemorate the voyage.

Prime Minister Stephen Harper apologizes to a crowd of 8,000 people at a festival in Surrey, BC, "on behalf of the government of Canada."

Timeline 97

Glossary

Cannery: A business that puts food into cans. Some Indian immigrants worked in the west-coast canneries in BC where fish, such as salmon, caught by local fishermen were put into cans.

Citizenship: The country that a person belongs to. When you are a citizen of a country, you can have a passport from the country and receive all the rights and benefits that the country offers.

Civil Rights: The basic privileges that come with being a member of society in a certain country. Things such as a right to vote, to have an education, and to receive justice in the courts are civil rights.

Coolie: A somewhat derogatory term that referred to manual or slave labour from Asia in the late nineteenth and early twentieth centuries.

Culture: The way of life of a group of people and how they interact with their surroundings. Culture is considered a distinguishing feature of a group, such as an ethnic group, but individuals within a culture can be diverse.

Delegation: A small group of people who represent a much larger group's ideas or demands.

Deportation: The sending away of people from the country where they are living back to the country from whence they came. For example, sending Indian activists living in Canada back to India.

Diaspora: The movement or spread of people away from their homeland.

Discrimination: Unjust actions that are caused by a particular mindset or prejudice; a means of treating people negatively because of their group identity. Discrimination may be based on age, ancestry, gender, language, race, religion, political beliefs, sexual orientation, family status, physical or mental disability, appearance, or economic status. Acts of discrimination hurt, humiliate, and isolate the victim.

Disenfranchised: Taking away someone's right to vote. Indo-Canadian citizens in British Columbia were disenfranchised in 1907. They were not allowed to vote in municipal, provincial, or federal elections until 1947.

Emigration: Leaving one's home country to go to a different country.

Ghadar Party: A political party formed by Punjabis in Canada and the US in the early 1900s to fight for independence for India. They were not against using violence, if necessary. Also spelled Gadar and Ghadr.

Gurdwara: This term means "Gateway to the Guru" and is the place of worship, or temple, for Sikhs.

Guru: A religious leader, or great teacher, in the Sikh religion. There were ten gurus in the history of Sikhism. The tenth, or final, guru died in 1709.

Head Tax: In an attempt to stop, or severely limit, immigration from China, the Canadian government levied the Chinese Head Tax in 1885. Each potential immigrant, including children, had to pay to come. The sum was too much for most immigrants, so they didn't come.

Hindoo: A generic term for all Indians in the late nineteenth and early twentieth centuries. The term was often used in newspaper articles about Indian immigrants, as well as in the general population. The term was racist and reflected the general population's lack of knowledge concerning Indian culture and religions.

Hindu: Commonly refers to a person who follows the religion of Hinduism, the third largest religion in the world. The majority of Hindus live in India.

Immigration: The arrival of people into a country from their homeland.

Injustice: A wrongful action taken against an individual or group that denies them their basic rights.

Islam: This is the world's second largest religion. Followers of Islam are called Muslims.

Khalsa: Followers of the Sikh religion are members of the Khalsa, or society of "pure ones." The Khalsa was created in 1699 by the last guru and those who accept it are known as Khalsa Warriors.

Mughal/Moghul Empire: The invading power from Persia (now Iran) that dominated life in India from 1526 to the mid 1800s.

Mutiny: The rising up of individuals or groups against the power of authority. In India, the rebellion of Indian soldiers against their British officers in 1857 is known as The Mutiny.

Nautch: This was a style of dance in India and its performers were known as nautch girls in the 1800s and 1900s.

Oppression: When the feelings, ideas, or demands of an individual or group of people are not recognized or allowed to be expressed by authorities, such as the government, justice system, police, or military.

Partition: In 1947, when India gained its independence from Britain, it was decided to divide India into two countries: India, mainly Hindu; and Pakistan, which would be mainly Muslim.

Prejudice: An attitude, usually negative, directed toward a person or group of people based on wrong or distorted information. Prejudiced thinking may result in acts of discrimination.

Punjab: A region in northern India where the Sikh religion originated. It was also inhabited by Hindus and Muslims. The Punjab was divided up during the partition of India in 1947.

Racism: A belief that one race is superior to another. People are not treated as equals because of their cultural or ethnic differences. Racism may be systemic (part of institutions, governments, organizations, and programs) or part of the attitudes and behaviour of individuals.

Redress: To right a wrong, sometimes by compensating the victim or by punishing the wrong-doer. Refers to the movement within the Indo-Canadian community for an official apology and payment for the injustices of the government's actions toward Indian immigrants in the early 1900s in general and for the Komagata Maru incident in particular.

Sepoy: An Indian soldier who served under the British in India from the 1600s onwards.

Sikh: A religious group, first established in the Punjab of India in the fifteenth century.

Singh: All male Sikhs take on the name "Singh" when they become members of the Khalsa.

Slavery: The ownership, buying, and selling of humans, mostly black Africans, as objects, mainly for labour. The slave trade was abolished everywhere in the Americas by 1888.

For Further Reading

Non-fiction Books:

Kazimi, Ali. *Undesirables: White Canada and the Komagata Maru - An Illustrated History*. Douglas & McIntyre, 2012.

▶ Watch Ali Kazimi discuss Canada's whites only immigration policy at tinyurl.com/komagata14

Johnston, Hugh. *The Voyage of the Komagata Maru: The Sikh Challenge to Canada's Colour Bar*. Delhi: Oxford University Press, 1979.

▶ Watch Professor Hugh Johnston talk about Canada's early immigration policy and how it was challenged by Gurdit Singh at tinyurl.com/komagata10

Jagpal, Sarjeet Singh. *Becoming Canadians: Pioneer Sikhs in their Own Words*. Harbour Publishing, 1994.

Singh, Baba Gurdit. *Voyage of the Komagata Maru or India's Slavery Abroad*. First published in Punjabi in 1928. English translation, Chandigargh, India: Unistar Books, 2007.

Malik, Tariq. *Chanting Denied Shores. An historical novel spanning seven years (1914–1921) in the lives of four protagonists of the Komagata Maru debacle*. For a summary, see www. bookclubbuddy.com/2011/chanting-denied-shores-by-tariq-malik/2011.

Films/Plays/Audio Recordings:

Breakaway, by Vinay Virmani. Directed by Robert Lieberman, 2011. A comedy about a young Sikh hockey team in Mississauga, Ontario. "Rajvinder Singh is struggling to balance the wishes of his traditional Sikh family and his own true passion for hockey. Raj and his friends play only for fun, held back by the prejudice and mockery of other teams as their turban-clad crew steps onto the ice. Enter Coach Dan Winters and soon the Speedy Singhs are competing in a real tournament . . ." See www.reelcanada.com/films/breakaway for more details.

Continuous Journey, by Ali Kazimi. TV Ontario, 2004. This award-winning feature documentary investigates the events surrounding the Komagata Maru. Mr. Kazimi is an associate professor in the Department of Film at York University.

The Komagata Maru: A Voyage of Shattered Dreams, by Sushma Datt. Komagata Maru: Continuing the Journey, Jan 1, 1989.

▶ Watch an excellent overview of the history of Indian immigration to Canada and the story of the Komagata Maru at tinyurl.com/komagata11

"The Komagata Maru Incident, a Play" by Sharon Pollock in *Six Canadian Plays* (first edition) ed. Tony Hamill, Playwrights Canada Press, Toronto 1992, pp. 229-286.

▶ Hear Sharon Pollock's story of how she came to write her play at tinyurl.com/komagata17

Komagata Maru, by Deepa Mehta, to be released in 2014. Funded by the Government of Canada. "Komagata Maru is based on a true story surrounding the voyage of a Japanese ship by the name 'Komagata Maru' hired by people from Punjab led by Gurdit Singh from Hong Kong to Vancouver in 1914 with 376 passengers on board seeking a new life in the promised land. The film also depicts the martyrdom of Mewa Singh."

Websites:

Komagatamarujourney.ca — A comprehensive website created through Simon Fraser University. It includes text, photographs and documents, video interviews, detailed reference lists, interactive timeline, passenger lists, biographies, glossary, and lesson plans for teachers.

Sikhpioneers.org — An American website that has a section on the Komagata Maru, a list of references, and many good photos.

asia-canada.ca/home — A website by Historica Canada containing many articles and images of the struggle of Asians who have immigrated to Canada in the past, as well as current immigration policies and attitudes.

www.canadiansikhheritage.ca/en/node/10 — A website devoted to exploring different aspects of Sikh-Canadian heritage including research on Sikhism, Passage to Canada, Khalsa Diwan Society Abbotsford, and the Sikh Heritage Museum.

vancouverhistory.ca/archives_komagatamaru.htm — A database highlighting the work done to digitize the articles from the Vancouver Daily News Province concerning South Asian Migration during the years 1906–1915.

▶ **WATCH THE VIDEO**

Look for this symbol throughout the book for links to video clips available on the website *Komagata Maru: Continuing the journey,* at www.komagatamarujourney.ca

Visual Credits

A Selective Collection of Hong Kong Historic Postcards, Hong Kong: Joint Publishing Co., 1993: p. 49 (top right)

Abbey, MCpl Angela, Canadian Forces Combat Camera: p. 78–9, 79 (top)

Asian Journal, Volume 1, Issue 25; December 17, 2010: p. 91 (bottom)

Ardizzone, Edward. *Indian Diary 1952-53.* London: The Bodley Head, 1984. p. 11 (bottom): p. 16 (centre right)

Baron and Baroness John Bachofen von Echt, private collection: p. 10

Bellingham's American, Woodring College of Education, 1907 Sept 5: p. 38 (top)

Breakaway Productions: p. 86 (bottom)

British Columbia Legislature: p. 90 (top left)

Canada Post Corporation, 1999: p. 93 (bottom)

Canadian Press: p. 85 (bottom)

CFB Esquimalt Naval and Military Museum: p. 60 (centre)

Central Sikh Museum: p. 73 (bottom)

Chand, Arjan Singh. *Komagata Maru scrapbook.* 1914: p. 57 (right)

Chouhan, Raj: p. 82 (bottom)

Chung Collection, UBC Library: p. 20 (bottom)

Citizenship and Immigration Canada: p. 80 (bottom)

City of Vancouver Archives: p. 23 (bottom, Port P1551), 30–31 (Van-Sc-P122), 31 (CVA 660-348), 33 (bottom, P1067), 38 (right, CVA 99-3105), 39 (top 509D7f1_040), 50–51 (CVA 7-122), 54 (bottom, CVA 7-129), 55 (bottom, CVA 7-133), 56 (CVA 7-132), 58–59 (centre, Pan N151), 58–59 (top, 509D7f1_040), 68 (bottom, CVA 300-24), 69 (left, CVA 1184-1572)

Cleveland Beach, Milo. *The New Cambridge History of India: Mughal and Rajput Painting.* Cambridge: Press Syndicate of the University of Cambridge, 1992: p. 8.

Dance, Nathaniel. *Lord Clive.* London, National Portrait Gallery: p. 14 (bottom)

Fischer, Louis. *The Life of Mahatma Gandhi.* New York: Harper & Row, 1983: p. 19 (bottom), 70 (right)

Freer Gallery of Art, Smithsonian Institution, Washington, DC: p. 9 (top)

Ghadarite poems, Bancroft Library, University of California Berkeley, CA: p. 46 (top left)

Gibbs, Philip. *India Our Eastern Empire.* London: Cassell and Company, Ltd., 1903: p. 17 (top)

Guha, Ramachandra. *India After Gandhi.* New York: HarperCollins, 2007: p. 68 (right)

Hayes, Derek. *Canada: An Illustrated History.* Toronto: Douglas and MacIntyre, 2004: p. 21 (centre & bottom), 37 (left), 39 (left)

Hayward, Jonathan: p. 79 (bottom)

Hickman, Angela, personal collection: p. 84–85, 87 (right), 94 (bottom)

Hou, Charles and Cynthia. *Great Canadian Political Cartoons 1820 to 1914.* Vancouver: Moddy's Lookout Press, 1997: p. 21 (top), 38 (left), 50 (left), 58 (left), 61 (top left)

House of Commons Collection, Ottawa: p. 82 (top), 83 (top), 83 (bottom)

Hudson Collection, Cambridge South Asian Archive: p. 14 (centre)

India Office Library: p. 15 (bottom), 17 (bottom)

Indian Museum, Calcutta: p. 16 (bottom)

Innes, Jack. "Such is life." 1914 June 5: p. 41 (top)

———. 1914, May 30. Protecting his own!: p. 49 (bottom right)

James, Lawrence. *Raj: British India.* New York: Little, Brown, and Co., 1998: p. 13 (left and right), 15 (centre)

Kalwant Singh Nadeem Parmar, private collection: p. 45 (bottom), 62, 65 (top)

Khalsa Diwan Society, Vancouver: p. 67 (top), 69 (right)

Komagata Maru Committee of Inquiry. March 1915: p. 64 (top & bottom)

Lambert, Earl (1914, June 2). So near and yet so far. Vancouver Daily Province: p. 51 (centre)

Leidenfrost, Wayne / Province: p. 80 (right, M-PRV0611KHALSA)

Les Baszo / Province: p. 81 (top, PRV0407Nvaisakhi12), 84 (bottom left, PRV0407Nvaisakhi07)

Library and Archives Canada: p. 37 (right, C-004650), 42 (left, C-006597)

Martin Stainforth, private collection: p. 12 (left and right)

McGill University, McCord Museum, Notman Photographic Archives: p. 42 (right)

Metropolitan Toronto Police Museum: p. 25 (top)

Miller, Carman. *Canada's Little War.* Toronto: James Lorimer & Co., 2003: p. 24 (bottom), 25 (right)

Museum of Vancouver, Major J.S. Matthews Collection: p. 58–59 (bottom, H982.217.104)

National Archives of Canada: p. 47 (bottom MIKAn134838)

National Library of Jamaica Special Collections, Baillie Collection, courtesy of: p. 18

———, Valdez Collection: p. 19 (top)

Nolan, E.H., ed. *The History of India and of The British Empire in the East, vol. 1.* London: Virtue & Co. Ltd., 1878: p. 9 (right), 10 (bottom)

———. *The History of India and of The British Empire in the East, vol. 5.* London: Virtue & Co. Ltd., 1878: p. 10 (bottom)

O'Brien, Lucius. In *Toronto to 1918. An Illustrated History,* by J.M.S. Careless Toronto: James Lorimer, 1984: p. 24 (top)

Office of the Hon. Tim Uppal, MP, Edmonton-Sherwood Park: p. 83 (bottom)

Office of Nina Grewel: p. 92–93

Parliamentary Library of Canada: p. 90 (top right), 91 (top left), 91 (top right)

Radio Times Hulton Picture Library: p. 14 (top)

Rainford, Sara. Rainfoto Photography: p. 81 (bottom), 84 (top), 86 (left & centre top), 94 (top), 95 (top), 95 (middle)

Raj Pal Gulati, personal collection: p. 74 (bottom)

Roy, Patricia and John Herd Thompson, eds. *British Columbia, Land of Promises.* Toronto: Oxford University Press, 2006: p. 27 (bottom, NAC PA122652), 29 (top)

Royal Academy of Arts, London: p. 11 (centre)

Royal BC Museum, images courtesy of: p. 28 (top, e_05027 & bottom, i_61147), 29 (bottom, g_03515), 32 (bottom, a_09159), 34 (bottom, i_68722), 35 (right f_06583), 53 (centre, d_06735), 55 (centre, d_05577), 61 (bottom, d_07570)

Seattle Art Museum, Seattle, WA: p. 9 (bottom)

SFU Library: p. 40 (top, Box4_335B_0001), 41 (bottom, 509D7f1), 43 (top left, 509D7f8_028), 44 (bottom, Mining_Certificate), 47 (top, Box6_347), 51 (top, Cartoonn_0006), 53 (bottom, Passenger_list_03), 67 (right, Box1_168A_0001), 71 (Box4_233B_001), 88 (Poem_0001), 89 (top, P1012695 & P1012696), 90 (middle, HarperApology_0003), 93 (middle, Play_english), 95 (bottom, Nee1013_0001)

———, IndoCanadian Collection, Bennett Library: p. 66 (bottom)

Singh, Dr. Amrik: p. 46 (inset)

Singh, Gurdit. *Slavery Abroad.* Chandigarh, India: Unistar Books, 2007: p. 19 (centre), 34 (bottom left), 49 (top left), 55 (top), 63, 93 (top)

Singh, K.K., C.F. Andrews and Kartan Singh Hundal. Indians in Canada, 1920: p. 65 (bottom)

Singh, S. *Souvenir of Darjeeling.* © S. Singh: p. 16 (top), 17 (left)

Singh, Teja. *Letter to J. H. MacGill:* p.20 (top)

Singh Japal, Sarjeet. *Becoming Canadians: Pioneer Sikh in their Own Words.* Madeira Park, BC: Harbour Publishing, 1994: p. 21 (top), 32 (top), 43 (bottom left & bottom right), 45 (centre), 46 (bottom left & top right), 65 (centre), 66 (top), 67 (left), 68 (top), 69 (right), 70 (left), 75 (bottom left)

Smith, Ian. *Vancouver Sun:* p. 80 (left, SUN0308NReyat04)

Tiwana, Jagpals. *The Maritime Sikh Society Origin and Growth:* p. 76, 77 (top & bottom)

University of British Columbia Library, Rare Books & Special Collections, Japanese Canadian Photograph Collection: p. 41 (centre, JCPC 36.011)

University of Washington Libraries, Special Collections: p. 22 (bottom, UW18745), 30 (bottom left, UW15673)

van Manen, Mark / Vancouver Sun: p. 89 (bottom, M-Sun0522n Maru2)

Vancouver City Album. Toronto: Douglas and Macintyre, 1991: p. 25 (left), 26, 27 (top & centre), 37 (top), 57 (left), 75 (top left, top right, bottom right)

Vancouver Public Library: p. 43 (top right), 48 (#6231), 53 (top, #6228)

———, BC Multicultural Portrait Collection: p. 34–35, 40 (bottom), 74 (left), 87 (left)

———, Special Collections: p. 22–23 (VPL 9426), p. 33 (top, VPL 83421), 34 (top left, VPL 86540), 43 (top right, VPL_photo_009), 45 (top, VPL 7641), 49 (bottom left, VPL 13162), 52 (top, VPL 121 & bottom, VPL 119), 54 (top, VPL 136), 57 (bottom, VPL 13161), 59 (VPL 122), 60 (right, VPL 128 & top, VPL 123), 73 (top, VPL 46227)

Watson, Francis. *A Concise History of India.* New York: Charles Scribner's Sons, 1975: p. 11 (top), 14 (top), 72 (top & bottom)

Yee, Paul. *Chinatown.* Toronto: James Lorimer & Co. Ltd., 2005: p. 36

Wiki public domain: p. 44 (right), p. 85 (top)

Vancouver Sun: p. 52–53 (June 26, 1914), 61 (July 25, 1914), 85 (bottom, Ian Smith/The Canadian Press)

Index